SUCCESS HABITS
OF
HIGH ACHIEVERS

DEVELOP HIGH PERFORMANCE HABITS, SENSE OF URGENCY, PROBLEM SOLVING SKILLS, AND ACHIEVE YOUR GOALS

VISHAL PANDEY

TABLE OF CONTENTS

INTRODUCTION

This is not a just book about success tips from high achievers. This is a book about fundamentals. The proven concepts & exercises can be used to achieve any goal you may have.

There is a lot of information in it, and applicable at different times during your journey to success.

For example, if your goal is to start a new business, you'll need a belief that you *can* do it, along with high motivation and a plan of action. It would be best to refer to chapter 3, chapter 4 and chapter 6.

When you make further progress and face obstacles such as slow progress, fear of rejection/failure, and loss of focus & discipline... it would be best to re-read chapter 9 and chapter 8 which thoroughly deal with these issues.

If your goal is to lose 10 pounds weight, you will again need to start with a strong belief that you *can* do, along with high motivation and a plan of action.

And after making some progress, you may face obstacles like not able to lose the last five pounds, fear of failure, lack of discipline. Refer to chapter 8 and 9.

This book embodies habits, routines, mindset, and skills of top businessmen, athletes, musicians, and other world class performers to achieve *any* goal you may have. Whether you want to:

- Start a new business
- Increase your income
- Lose weight
- Learn a new skill
- Find a better job
- Increase your confidence
- Get better marks in exams
- Become more social
- Increase your productivity
- Worry less & be happy

The fundamentals in *Success Habits of High Achievers* will show you how to achieve all your dreams in the most efficient manner. Once you implement the key concepts, you will achieve success after success in *all* areas of life.

This book is divided into 10 parts. Different segments of the book are meant to be useful at different stages of your journey. Take note of the problem you are currently facing and refer to the section of the book which deals with that specific issue.

We will dive into every single aspect of achieving success in great detail. You will learn real-life techniques, habits & mindset of the very best in the world.

The information contained in *Success Habits of High Achievers* is universally applicable but the *'key'* lies in its application. If you take time to learn the principles and apply them, they will continue to serve you forever.

Some people say "I got it" even before mastering these principles. Please don't make that mistake. Apply these principles until they become a part of who you are.

Even then you may need to come back and re-read the book because 1) you might have missed some information during your initial read-through and 2) it re-introduces the parts you might have forgotten.

All the best,

Vishal Pandey

Chapter #1

LAYING THE FOUNDATION

"You can't build a tall building on a weak foundation" - **Gardon B. Hinckley,** winner of Presidential Medal of Freedom - the highest civilian award of the United States.

Like everything in life, success comes at a price. It takes a lot of sweat & tears to achieve something. Most people understand why hard work is required for success and they believe they can do it. However, after a good start they face their first obstacle, then a second, then a third, fourth, fifth, sixth and so on...

Heartwarming, right?

It takes a lot of physical as well as mental fortitude to overcome the challenges you are going to face on your journey to success. So before we start out all guns blazing, we *need* a strong foundation.

"There are no shortcuts to building a team each season. You build the foundation brick by brick" - **Bill Belichick**, the legendary NFL coach.

Many people quit before they reach their goals. Their reasons may be different - "I can't do it" or "I don't have the time" or "It will not work" etc, but one thing is common. They lack a strong foundation.

I also was like this for a long time. Interesting thing was, I didn't know I had a weak foundation. In fact, I didn't even know what foundation was!

I clearly remember the time when I & my friend Dev were looking for a new job. We were young and left our first job recently, pretty confident that we would find a new one in a matter of days. Of course, it turned out to be a *lot* harder than we expected. The competition for open vacancies was overwhelming. Applied for jobs online, but never got a reply from any employer. Our contacts too were not able to help us, "Vishal, we will let you know if there are any open vacancies."

I bet all you job-hunt veterans are smiling right now.

Well, it was pretty hard.

I even had a decent knowledge about how to achieve goals, because reading personal achievement literature was my hobby at that time. Still, it was tough.

Dev got fed up after two months. He went back to his hometown and joined his family business.

I tried many different things. Read different books, listened to audio programs - basically anything I could get my hands on - until I realized something is missing. And without that 'something', landing a new job was going to be quite difficult.

After a close examination, two basic principles came up, which serve as the foundation for achieving success in *any* area of life. Since then, a lot has changed. I got the job I was looking for but didn't stop there. I moved on to other goals but the foundation still retains its importance.

Whenever I start neglecting the foundation, my results start going downhill *fast*!

"Building a business is like building a home. If the foundation rests on an unstable setting or is constructed with subpar materials, it doesn't matter if the rest of the home is perfect. It will never be a joy to its owner." - **Thomas J. Stanley**, multiple-award winning author of *"The Millionaire Next Door."*

A tree can grow only as high as its roots are strong. If the roots are strong, the tree can grow high. But if the roots are weak, the tree will bend and fall.

The foundation you're about to discover will serve you in all important areas of life - work, relationships, health, finances, love, and even spirituality. Whatever you may want, it must be built upon this foundation.

On initial impression, the two foundations may seem simple. But look around, people usually downplay the importance of these two factors. It is commonly thought that having motivation is enough to achieve your goals. I have tried that and watched others do the same, only to get run out of fuel later.

I have learned to never underestimate the importance of foundation.

During your journey to success, you will face several challenges. To overcome these challenges, you must build a solid foundation. An earthquake can easily crumble a building with a weak base. But if the foundation is strong, it will remain standing after the earthquake has passed.

Foundation #1

POSITIVE ATTITUDE

"Optimism is essential to achievement and it is also the foundation of courage and true progress" - **Nicholas M. Butler**, Nobel Peace Prize Winner (1931)

Having a Positive attitude is the first foundation of success and a shining characteristic of every successful person I have met and read about.

I still remember when I used to read about the importance of a positive attitude and think - "yeah, yeah. I know."

But in my mind, I didn't give too much thought to it.

Now after thirteen years of massive successes and failures, I am completely convinced that a positive Attitude is *everything*. Every action we take is determined by our attitude. Positive attitude reinforces positive actions, which moves you in the right direction, while a negative attitude does the opposite.

Why do you think Dev quit before finding a new job, while I kept searching? We both were equal in all aspects - education, age, culture, background, society etc.

The difference was in attitude.

When I faced rejections, my focus was on finding the *solution* of the problem – how to improve my presentation, C.V., body language and communicate how I fulfilled their requirement. It did that because I *saw* a bright future. I *believed* in my dream.

Dev had to deal with the same challenges, but he did not see sunshine behind the mountain. His focus was on the negative - how low the vacancies are, interviewers are unfriendly, and it's not going to work.

Dev, me, you and everyone else have the potential to achieve success in life. The difference lies in how we look at things. When a person sees challenges as 'impossible', he or she will feel powerless even *before* trying something.

"*Rock bottom became the solid foundation on which I rebuild my life*" - **J. K. Rowling**, billionaire & renowned author of *Harry Potter* series.

Success in any area of life requires a shift to a positive attitude.

In later chapters, you will discover several methods to deal with challenges you would face during your journey to success, but even they will be of no-use in absence of a positive attitude.

It is the canvas on which every beautiful painting of success is created.

The impact of a small shift...

Good news is, even the smallest shift in attitude can bring great results.

One of my friends used to struggle with being social in his office. He was an introvert by nature and had troubles opening up to new people. He always said, "I have nothing to talk about, and even if I did, they will not like me anyway." I sat down with him and convinced him to just say hello to people in his office and smile. He agreed because it was only a small shift in behavior.

The results were amazing. People were very receptive to his greetings and started conversations themselves. Initially, my friend was a bit nervous in conversations but it quickly became a habit. Now he is well known by his colleagues and has the reputation of a warm and social person.

A tiny shift in attitude gave such a great result.

"Your attitude, not your aptitude, will determine your altitude." - **Zig Ziglar**, world-renowned presenter, speaker & author.

In life, success and failure are only inches apart. A very small shift is needed to get either result. You must develop a positive attitude. It'll help you in several ways.

For more proof, look at people who are consistently at the top of their respective field - CEOs, successful entrepreneurs, world-famous actors, award-winning athletes, great singers, artists and professionals who have achieved success - all have a positive attitude in life.

If you read the autobiographies of famous people, who are considered 'greats' of their field, the importance of attitude becomes apparent. Nelson Mandela, Steve Jobs, Albert Einstein, Mahatma Gandhi, Mother Teresa, and countless other great people's stories are proof that whatever your aim, positive attitude will bring success and greatness, while negativity will lead to an inevitable downfall.

This is especially true in our modern, competitive world. Having a positive attitude is an edge. It gives you resilience to face the harshness of life. No matter how big your problems are, you are likely to succeed if you consciously see the positives in every challenge or failure.

For example, you aspire to improve your health. Know what, it's difficult. It takes discipline, self-control, and knowledge of nutrition & exercise. It's not an easy task. Same with improving your finances, social status, communication, relationships and every kind of goal you have.

If it is worth something, it won't be easy.

That is why having a positive attitude is a must. There will be times when you will feel like nothing is happening; all your time and effort is getting wasted. Your revenues are flat, you are not losing weight, you keep messing up at the same tune while learning guitar. It's in moments like these, positive attitude shows its true significance.

"*The greatest discovery of all time is that a person can change his future by merely changing his attitude.*" - **Oprah Winfrey**, American talk show host, actress and television producer.

With a positive attitude, you would keep going. You will have faith that there *is* a better future. Things will *definitely* improve if I put in time & effort.

I have seen so many talented, intelligent people quit around me after having just one or two setbacks, it blew my mind. Instead of learning from what did not work, they took it personally and stepped back.

This is caused due to lack of belief in the fact that the universe keeps track of the effort you have made and it'll not go in vain. Things will work out. They do work out. Believe it.

"*If you believe it'll work out, you'll see opportunities. If you believe it won't, you'll see obstacles.*" - ***Wayne Dyer***, world famous speaker and author of 21 *New York Times* bestsellers.

The reverse is also true. Look around and you will find that people who are negative, usually wind up being unsuccessful. Not only that but they lack the gratitude and general satisfaction in their life. Their relationships become toxic and eventually get destroyed.

Having a negative attitude is a sure shot way to 'lose' in the game of life.

And attitude is contagious. You must keep yourself away from the company of negative people. We all have few negative, 'emotional leech' people in our life. It's best to keep your distance away from them as much as possible.

I have identified some people like that in my life and minimized my interactions with them. One of my friends introduced me to Raj. At first, I liked him. But later when I started hanging out with him, I realized he was constantly complaining about everything. He could find fault in everything & everyone. No matter how I tried to be positive around him, his strong negative outlook overwhelmed me every time.

Soon 'I' started pointing out faults in things, which I don't normally do. My other friends started telling me that I was changing. I was not positive and upbeat as before. Then I realized how strongly people influence each other. I minimized my interactions with Raj. It was the biggest thing that helped me get back to feeling positive and upbeat.

How to develop a positive attitude?

Conversely, be near positive people. Watch how they talk, what they say, how they think. Expose yourself to positive people as much as possible.

"Associate yourself with people of good quality, for it is better to be alone than in bad company" - **Booker T. Washington,** American educator, author and advisor to Presidents of the United States.

It is a psychological fact that we become a combination of five people with whom we spend most of our time. Be around people who are successful, positive, grateful and our mind will start adopting their behavior automatically. We subconsciously absorb thinking of the other person, whether it is positive or negative. That's the way our brains are wired.

What to do if you can't find positive people around you?

Don't be discouraged if you can't find positive people to hang out with. I discovered that great books, audio, video programs etc., all count towards changing your mind to be positive. It's not only about the surrounding people. It's about the top five "influences" that affect you on daily basis.

Reading a book by someone who is massively successful *will* influence your mind to think like them. As you continually read, watch or listen to top individuals, you will gradually begin to adopt their beliefs and mindsets, which would be *really* helpful if you can't find people like that in your actual life.

One of the biggest benefits of having a positive attitude is that it changes your focus from "surviving" to "thriving". Have you noticed people who are just coping through life? Their whole motivation is to just "get by". For them, having just enough to survive is fine.

With the right attitude, you will see situations and people differently. Your focus will be on what's good and what's possible. There will be aliveness inside you which other people will notice. You will have more passion and zest for life. You'll see challenges and difficulties merely as a stepping stone to success.

"Be the one thing you think you cannot do. Fail at it. Try again. Do better the second time. The only people who don't tumble at the high wire are those who never mount the high wire" - **Oprah Winfrey,** American talk show host, actress and television producer.

Imagine yourself on a boat in the middle of a lake. The boat is your attitude and the shores on either side are success and failure. If your attitude is right, you will move towards the shore of success. If you embrace negativity, you will move in the opposite direction, failure.

Some people ask me whether it is possible to change course if you have been moving in the wrong direction. My answer: I firmly believe it's *never* too late to change. You can always change at any point in your life. Take the example of Colonel Sanders who founded KFC *after* the age of 60.

There are countless examples of people who changed their destiny after the age of 50, 60, 70. It'll be a little tough because you are late to the party, but it's 100% POSSIBLE. Many people, like you, have changed their life.

It's never too late...

A great start would be to force yourself to find one positive quality in people and situations. Combine this with minimizing your exposure to negativity and spending time with positive people & books. You will experience rapid shifts in your thinking and attitude. In research done by Harvard Institute, researchers have found that technical knowledge is only fifteen percent of success. The rest of the eight five percent comes from having the right attitude and thinking.

I can personally vow for the importance of the right attitude and mindset because I have seen the *difference* they made in my life and other people's lives.

That is why this chapter is at the beginning of the book.

A positive attitude is one of the two pillars behind success.

Foundation #2

HEALTH

Let me introduce you to the second foundation of success - Health. The importance of good health cannot be understated, but many people seem to ignore this basic component of achieving success.

"*Your health is your starting point. Without it, you have nothing.*" **- Sienna Guillory,** Hollywood star and former model.

Achieving success by its very nature demands a sustained expenditure of energy over time. There are no shortcuts to success. It's a long, linear path filled with challenges and setbacks. And to successfully overcome these obstacles, we need a good reservoir of physical and mental energy.

Every top performing athlete takes adequate rest before the competition because they have a deep understanding of the fact that energy is the *key* to success. This is true for any kind of success, not just in sports.

Having good health will provide the following benefits:

1. Increased energy

Exercise directly affects our energy level. Deep breathing during exercise stimulates blood flow, which carries oxygen to every cell of the body. This transferred energy allows cells to create energy. As a result, we feel energized all day long.

2. Fat loss

Exercise our rate of metabolism. After exercise, our body continues to burn calories all day long. If the exercise was intense, the metabolic rate may increase until the next 48 hours. This means the body burns more calories even when you are sitting.

Fat reserves in the body are nothing but stored energy. Increased metabolism causes the body to start using fat reserves for energy, which causes fat loss. Fitness experts recommend exercise as an indispensable part of any fat loss program.

3. Stronger immune system

Daily exercise will make you more resistant against diseases ranging from common cold to cancer. While researchers are yet to scientifically prove a direct link between exercise and a strong immune system, it is generally accepted that exercise is one of the core pillars of health.

People who exercise have much a lower rate of catching ailments and are healthier than people who don't.

4. Removes toxins from the body

Exercise has a very strong detoxing effect on the body. During exercise, the lymph system gets activated which is a major detox system of the body. It cleans out all the waste proteins & toxins produced by cells. Other important detox organs are the colon, liver, and skin.

Colon & liver, aided by exercise, get rid of the toxins from the body continuously. Skin is the largest organ of the body. The sweating process during exercise helps remove toxins from the pores of our skin.

5. Better body shape

The human body is designed to move by nature. When we sit for hours at work, we are doing the opposite of what our bodies are designed to do. We are built to move, walk, run and then sleep when we need rest.

Our body is designed to stand straight or lie down flat on the ground. Sitting is not our default posture. However, in modern society, we spend most of our day sitting which causes spinal problems and other health issues.

The solution here is to exercise regularly. When we exercise, our body gets an opportunity to do what it was originally designed for. It leads to numerous benefits related to posture, energy, bone structure, and overall better health.

6. Feeling great all day long

Exercise puts you in a good mood due to increased secretion of 'feel good' chemicals in the body like endorphin, dopamine, and serotonin. Additionally, the increased core temperature of the body leads to relaxed muscles, which lower anxiety and stress levels.

Deep breathing during exercise makes your mind calm and relaxed. You become more focused and energized. Exercise stimulates growth of neurons in parts of the brain which are damaged by stress and depression.

A Study in 2010 found that three sessions of yoga per week resulted in increased secretion of GABA, a hormone related to improving mood and lifting depression. Results established exercise as one of the best things you can do to protect yourself from anxiety and depression.

7. Stronger muscles

Regular exercise leads to stronger muscles. When you exercise, muscles in the body break down. When you rest, your body repairs the broken muscles using protein and other nutrients.

But here, something new happens. While in the repairing process, body 'over-compensates' and increases the mass of muscles to avoid a breakdown in the future. This is the core concept behind muscle growth.

A lack of exercise results in degradation of muscles. Athletes work out even in the off-season just to maintain their existing muscles. Increased blood flow produced by exercise keeps muscles healthy and flexible.

8. Prevent Osteoporosis

Exercise, along with a nutritious diet, leads to stronger bone structure. Activities such as walking, running, weight lifting and yoga help maintain bone density, thus preventing Osteoporosis.

Numerous studies show a link between healthy bode structure and regular exercise. Just make sure to start slow. Don't put too much pressure on your joints & back. Take a healthy diet.

9. Lowers risk of heart attack

Exercise lowers your blood pressure which leads to reduced risk of heart attack. Optimized blood flow caused by exercise helps lower cholesterol levels and also prevents clotting inside arteries.

10. Lowers risk of Alzheimer's disease

Frequent exercise protects the brain from chronic diseases like Alzheimer's. It provides additional protection to Hippocampus, which is one of the first regions of the brain affected by Alzheimer's. In the year 2000, Dutch researchers have found that the people who are working out are 4 times less likely to develop the disease than people who don't work out.

By looking at the benefits, the importance of exercise is self-explanatory.

While there are a few examples of 'successful people' who don't take good care of their health, they are in such a minority that I call them outliers. They are not the rule. They are the exception.

I personally know a successful businessman like that. He does not care much about his health but he is doing quite well financially. At first glance, it may appear that things are going well for him, but when looked closely, he appears to be dissatisfied with how things are.

He told me that before achieving success in his business, he was healthy, energetic and full of vitality. It played a big part in the growth of his business. But once he thought he made it, he began to take things 'easy'.

He started skipping gym sessions and began indulging in high-fat foods containing sugar and salt. This combined with the fact he was sitting idle on a chair all day, his health began to go down.

Deteriorating health worsened his mood. He started becoming angry & frustrated frequently and began losing his focus and concentration. As a result, his work suffered and business slowly began to go down.

After suffering losses for months straight, he realized the root cause behind it was his poor health. It negatively affected the quality of his decisions, performance and leadership ability. He started eating healthy and joined the gym again. He said he could feel the difference in himself, and consequently, his business.

"If you have health, you probably will be happy, and if you have health and happiness, you have all the wealth you need, even if it is not all you want." **- Elbert Hubbard,** American writer, philosopher and the founder of Roycroft artisan community, New York.

No matter how rich & successful you may become, your health will always be your most important asset. It is the foundation for everything else you have in life: relationships, money, fun, travel, enjoyment, satisfaction, relaxation, passion and every other part of life there is, depends on your health.

It allows us to experience all those wonderful moments. Without good health, life loses its flair. So start treating your health as the *most* valuable asset you have and you'll be rewarded with unbelievable life experience.

Basic pointers for maintaining good health

1. Eat clean

Think of food as fuel for the body, and you would want good quality fuel inside your body. Start by adding more fresh fruits and vegetables in your diet. Don't worry too much about cutting down bad foods. I found that if you start adding more healthy food in your diet, the quantity of bad food decreases by itself.

Reduce your sugar intake as much as you can. Stop eating fried, deep cooked, or barbecued foods. Try olive oil for cooking. It's a much healthier alternative to normal cooking oils. Make sure you are taking omega-3 oil as well, for its numerous benefits. Add a green salad with every meal. Eat foods with low G.I., which stabilize your blood sugar and provide energy all day long. Search "low G.I. foods" in Google for a detailed list of low G.I. foods.

Eat the right kinds of carbohydrates. Shift from simple carbs to complex carbs, which break down slowly in the body, giving you a steady flow of energy throughout the day. You don't need much protein. The recommended amount is - 0.8 grams per kilograms of your body weight in a day. And while it's possible to get all the 20 different kinds of proteins entirely from plant sources (plenty of info available in books & Internet), it'll be a little tough. You can add a small amount of dairy or clean meats like chicken to your main fruits and vegetable diet. This will ensure that you get the whole range of amino acids easily.

If you eat a balanced diet with a wide range of fruits and vegetables, there will be enough vitamins and minerals included in your diet. Search online for the recommended quantity of vitamins & minerals per day. You should easily be meeting these requirements if you follow the guidelines above. If not, then consult your doctor for a good vitamin & mineral supplement. It will do wonders for your health and well being.

2. Drink enough water

Water makes up about 50-60% of our body. It is inside our cells, blood, tissues and other parts of the body. A lot of body processes (like sweating) make us lose water fast. Sweating alone can use up to half liter water in an hour. In extreme weather, that amount can rise to two liters of water consumed in an hour.

Even a 2% decrease in total water content level of the body, reduces our ability to perform at peak mental and physical level. If you continue to push on without drinking water, you will start getting irritable and tired, along with higher chances of getting muscle cramps. 5% decrease in total water level of the body cause extreme fatigue and drowsiness. It may cause altered vision and tingling sensation in the whole body. 10-15% loss in water levels cause wrinkles on the skin and muscles malfunction. Any loss greater than that is often fatal.

Such is the importance of water for our health. Drink at least 2 to 4 liters of water daily depending on the weather conditions you are living in and the amount of physical activity you do. The more extreme the weather, the more water you need to preserve your water level. Drinking 2 to 4 liters of water is considered safe by many experts. Consult your physician to know exactly how much do you need based on your unique condition.

3. Exercise

It is quite well known that exercise is good for our health. Less known is the *type* of exercise we need and its duration. Research shows that for the majority of people a 15-minute brisk walk (walking at around 6 km/hr) is the ideal exercise, as it's not too stressful on the body and pumps up the oxygen flow nicely.

It is one of the few physical activities you can do all your life. Even older people can take a brisk walk easily. The younger you start, the more benefits you get in the long term. No matter what your age, it's better to start exercising if you aren't already doing so. At a young age, the body can withstand heavy, rigorous physical activities. People in their 20s & 30s usually think about the gym and weight training whenever physical activity is mentioned.

For achieving optimum health, heavy exercises are not absolutely necessary. Here are some simple exercises which are great for your health:

- Brisk walk

- Cycling at slow speed

- Sweeping or raking outside lawn

- Gardening

- Table tennis

- Painting & plastering

- Heavy house cleaning

- Light dancing

- Push-ups, sit-ups with moderate effort

It all depends on the effort you are willing to make and your physical condition. If you decide to take exercises like walking or cycling, one important point to note is you burn the same number of calories for covering a fixed distance.

For example, if you walk faster for 10 miles, you will burn a lot of calories initially but will slow down afterward. If you walk slowly, you will burn lesser calories but keep doing that longer.

In the end, whatever your speed is, you end up burning the same amount of calories for covering a fixed distance. As always, consult your physician before starting any new physical exercise.

4. Adequate sleep

One of the most important things for your health is getting enough sleep. When you are well-slept, your mind is much sharper, alert and resilient. You will have more energy & focus which would increase your overall performance during the day.

On the other hand, when you are not well slept, you will feel drowsy and irritable all day. Your willpower will decrease and your emotions will be all over the place. You would become prone to indulging in instant stimulation (like TV, alcohol) which would eat up all your time. Sleep is one of those things which can either make or break your day. It is important to get proper sleep at night.

But how much sleep is enough?

It depends on the individual. Every one of us is unique and has a different sleep pattern. Some people can function normally on 6 hours of sleep while others may need 8-9 hours to feel well-rested.

However, research on sleep shows that most people need 7 to 8 hours of proper sleep for optimum health and functioning. I personally need around 7.5 - 8 hours of sleep. When I am well-slept, I feel refreshed and energized all day.

Try getting up at different times to find your own unique sleep requirement. You would eventually end up somewhere between 7 to 8:30 hours. Whatever your need is, get that many hours of sleep every day.

Don't be afraid of losing your productivity time. Some people think sleeping 8 hours is a waste of time. Actually, you will be a LOT more productive. You will have increased energy & mental alertness throughout the day. That one hour of extra sleep will result in several hours of increased performance. It's a worthy trade-off.

One more thing. It's not just the quantity of sleep which is important. "Quality" is also critical. A few pointers on improving the quality of your sleep:

- Don't eat a heavy meal late at night.

- Avoid computer and mobile screens, TV, and bright lights one hour before sleep.

- Do relaxing activities before bed. Read a book, write journal etc.

- Keep the temperature of the bedroom cool and comfortable.

- Invest in good quality mattress and pillows.

- Fix a time to sleep.

- Sleep in a completely dark room. Even dim light can interfere in the quality of sleep.

Note: you should consult your physician before making any changes in your diet, exercise or lifestyle. Each one of us has our own unique physical and mental condition and benefit from more personalized advice. The pointers given above are general guidelines for good health, but professional medical advice should always be your first priority.

Get your health in check. Without it, the road to success will be extremely hard. While it's certainly *possible* to reach success in-spite of having bad health, it will be an uphill battle. We want our health to be our advantage, not our liability. Make efforts to improve your health and the rewards would be incredible!

"It is health that is real wealth and not pieces of gold and silver" - **Mahatma Gandhi**, civil right leader.

Till now, we have covered the foundational aspects. From here onward, we will go deep into specific methods and techniques to achieve success in any goal you may have set for yourself.

Chapter #2

DREAMS WITH A DEADLINE

"The indispensable first step to getting things you want out of life is this: decide what you want" **- BEN STEIN,** American writer, lawyer, comedian and Emmy award-winning game show host.

The first step in achieving your goals is knowing exactly what you want. Sounds simple, right? But many times people are not very clear about what they want to accomplish. The ones who do, have a distinct edge. Having a *detailed* vision of what you want is simply THE most important thing for being successful.

This is where goal setting comes in.

A goal represents your desire or vision that you want to bring to reality. It could be either big or small, does not matter, but it must be something you REALLY, REALLY want. That's very important. If it's something you desire with absolute willingness, then it's worth going for.

It's shouldn't be like you 'kind of want it'...

When you say you want it, you must *really* mean it!

"If you want to be happy, set a goal that commands your thoughts, liberates your energy and inspires your hopes." - **Andrew Carnegie**, one of the richest industrialists in history.

So make sure your goal is something you are crazy about because properly selected goals have *tremendous* power. They will fill you with unlimited energy and enthusiasm. You'll take more action, show more resilience (when facing challenges) and your motivation would be a lot stronger.

Setting a goal is 'must have' for success. Even the best sharpshooters in the world cannot hit their target... if they have no target! Have you ever heard of *anyone* who became successful at *anything*, without making it their aim?

The secret behind the most successful people is they *focused* on their desired outcome for long periods of time and it took continuous, sustained effort to arrive at their destination.

Without a compelling goal to move towards, you will be like a ship without a destination. Look at top success coaches of the world like Anthony Robbins or Brian Tracy, the first thing they teach is to select a specific goal.

Success, by its very definition, represents achieving the desired outcome. When there is no outcome, there is no success.

Success is not possible without a goal.

If you don't have a fixed goal, your energy and focus would be all over the place because they would lack a direction. But when you get clear about what you want, all your scattered energy gets focused and directed to your target like a laser, cutting through every obstacle that stands in the way.

To really hammer this point home, let's look at one of my favorite examples of how goals can change our lives.

Jim Carrey's success story

During his struggling period as a young comedian in 1990, one night, Jim Carrey drove up his old Toyota over a hill in Los

Angeles and wrote himself a cheque of 10 million dollars, dated 1995. The notation line written in the cheque was "for acting services rendered".

Since then, he always kept it in his wallet. Even when he was struggling, every time he reached out to his wallet, it reminded him of his actual goal. It gave him the strength to go on.

As time passed, his situation began to change. By the year 1995, he not only had starred in movies but gave mega-hits like Dumb and Dumber, Ace Ventura: Pet Detective, The Mask, Liar-Liar. He achieved his goal of making 10 million dollars.

And never looked back since...

His success story stands as an inspiration for millions of people all over and is one of the best examples of the power of goal setting.

World's best goal seeking mechanism - your mind

Let's look at an amazing fact about the human brain - it is naturally equipped with a goal-seeking mechanism inbuilt. In NLP (Neuro-linguistic programming) terms this mechanism is called Reticular Activating System (RAS in short).

If you wish to see the research behind it, Google - "reticular activating system psychology"

There has been a lot of research done in this area. Studies show anytime you set a goal, your mind actively looks for ways to achieve it. You will start noticing small details, people and situations you would have ignored earlier.

For example, have you ever thought about buying a particular car, and suddenly you started seeing that car everywhere on the road?

What's going on here? Actually, things that you need are around you all the time, but your mind focuses on them only when it needs to. This biological phenomenon is well documented in Dr. Maxwell Maltz's bestselling book *'Psycho-cybernetics'*.

It's a groundbreaking book about goal-seeking mechanism located inside the human brain. If you haven't already, I highly recommend checking it out. It's one of the best books of its kind and helped millions of people change their mindset.

Dr. Maxwell, a plastic surgeon, found that some patients still see themselves as 'ugly' even when they no longer have any facial scar or deformity. He concluded that the mind of an individual has the power to change the perception of self and the surrounding environment.

He wrote extensively about how the mind affects the perception of an individual. But we will mainly focus on how it affects success & failure and learn to use it to our advantage.

Your brain has a 'servo mechanism' build in. It's a goal-seeking system, very similar to a modern missile or torpedo. Whenever a missile is given a target and launched, it looks for the shortest, fastest, most efficient route to its target. If the target moves or missile itself sways from its path, servo-mechanism inside missile makes small adjustments and it gets back on course.

Your mind works in the same fashion. Now it's widely believed that the human mind is the best problem-solving system in the world.

(And you were thinking that your brain isn't any good...)

It's a powerful gift, and when you learn to use it properly, the amount of success you can have is virtually unlimited.

Activating success part of your brain

"Our thoughts, our feelings, our dreams, our ideas are physical in the universe. That if we dream something, if we picture something, it adds a physical thrust towards realization that we can put into the universe." - **Will Smith**, leading Hollywood actor, producer & media personality.

Ok. How do you tap into this success mechanism built inside your mind? What is the process?

The first thing you need is a clearly defined goal. Be *very specific* about what you want and why. Your mind does not like ambiguity. It needs a detailed vision of your objective. Only then your success mechanism could be activated.

So take a piece of paper and write down in detail about what outcome you want.

Be as specific as you can. The more details, the better. Personally, when I wrote about all the things that I wanted, I filled up three pages of my notebook. You don't have to fill that many. The number of pages is not important. Just make sure you have enough details about your goal to create a *clear picture* in your mind.

For example, if you want a new home, don't just say "I want a big, well-designed house in a good location". That's too vague. Fill in details such as -

How big is the house? Sq. feet?

How is it designed?

Which color?

How is the paint quality?

What's the shape & size of the windows?

Front & back lawns?

Where is the car parking?

How is the neighborhood?

How is the weather in that area?

Quite or happening place?

Near to the market/ shopping mall?

What's it like from inside - decoration, color, paint, furniture, curtains?

How many rooms?

How's the kitchen?

And most importantly - how do you *feel* inside your new home?

Details like this form a very clear picture of your goal. It's our first step. It takes effort, but make sure you take the time to do this. This part is very important.

Now that we have a clear picture of what we want, the second step is to set a TIME LIMIT.

When will you achieve your desired outcome?

Having a fixed time frame is very important. It creates a sense of urgency and makes your goals appear *real*.

"*Goals are dreams with a deadline*" - **Napoleon Hill,** author of the classic "*Think and Grow Rich*".

Without a time frame, you'll not take your goals seriously. It'll always be something you would do "in the future" or when you have "enough time". Excuses like that can be countered by setting a time limit.

Go ahead. Put a date in front of your goals. This seemingly simple step is a *major* key to success.

After you have set a time limit, there is one more thing I would like you to know...

Focus on 'WHAT', and 'HOW' will appear

You are afraid that you don't know *how* you will achieve your goals. You have no clue, and there's no clear path visible at this moment.

That's fine. Don't let it stop you.

You don't need to know *how* you will achieve your goals at *this* moment. Just knowing *what* you want is enough! You'll figure out how to do it later... when you start taking action. As we discussed earlier, the human mind is the world's greatest problem-solving system. It will figure out *how*.

Right now, focus on being clear about what you want.

Just do this. Do not think about how you will achieve it.

I did not understand this concept when I started. I doubted if I could ever figure out a way to achieve some of my goals. They were outside my reality. But I kept on moving forward with whatever information I had at the time.

Later, I was quite surprised by the fact that I *could* figure it out. All of a sudden, solutions would pop up, or I would meet someone who moved me closer to my destination. I couldn't believe it at first. I thought it was pure luck. But after going through the process several times, I firmly believe that our minds are capable of finding a solution no matter how difficult the problem.

Later in this book, we'll uncover strategies that will help you reach your goals effectively. But generally speaking, your mind is quite capable of finding a solution to any problem you might face. It really is a wonderful gift.

Thomas Edison had failed 10,000 times before he finally invented the light bulb. He said all those mistakes and failures taught him lessons that helped him finally create the light bulb.

When he started out, he didn't know how he was going to make a light bulb. He started with whatever he knew and 'figured-it-out' later.

You must *trust* the process. Have faith that path will become clear when you become clear about *where* you want to go. If you can see your destination, you will find a path which would lead you there.

"Whatever we plant in our subconscious mind, and nourish it with repetition and emotion, will one day become a reality." -

Earl Nightingale, Hall of fame motivational speaker, radio presenter & author.

Believe in yourself and your dreams. Because people who don't, tend to give up even before they take their first step. If you any successful person's autobiography, you will find they did not know *how* they would achieve their goals initially. But they had trust and kept on going... 'how' became apparent along the way.

That is the way every great achiever obtains success. Let's take another example.

Walt Disney dreamed of a wonderful place where people would go and forget all their worries. He had an amazing vision, but no money.

To fund Disneyland, he approached ten banks, but they turned down his application. He approached another ten banks, and they turned him down too. After many other rejections, most people would have quit. But he didn't.

He tried different approaches, speeches, and presentations. Finally, one bank was able to see his vision and agreed to fund Disneyland, but it took Walt Disney 300 rejections to get it done! He was rejected by 300 banks before he got 1 to agree.

That's called trust. He had no idea how he was going to arrange funds, but he kept going, and most importantly, didn't give up when times were hard. He had a firm belief that he was going to make it. Disneyland wasn't just his dream, it was a dream for the world.

And now Disneyland is a reality.

It stands there as a beacon of joy and happiness for the whole world because the man who envisioned it didn't quit.

You have to do the same. Take the first step. Your journey will show you the path. Don't be afraid. Have faith in the process.

You WILL figure out a way.

Just take the first step.

How to set goals?

Now let's dive into goal setting. It's important to get this step right. When you set the right goals, you have unlimited energy and motivation to succeed.

Let's start from the base - what do you want?

No. What do you REALLY, REALLY, REALLY want?

Ideally, your goals should make you feel humbled at the thought of achieving them. Whenever you think about them, you should feel a shiver down your spine. You should feel crazy amounts of desire, excitement, and joy.

These are the kind of goals worth going for...

When you set modest goals, your emotions will not be there (believe me, 90% of your success comes from managing your emotions. More on that later). But when you set goals which make you feel excited, that's a major success in itself.

You will give your 100% to obtain it because it feels so compelling.

Some people ask me - Should I set smaller (but easily achievable) goals because I am not certain if I could achieve my bigger goals? My answer - it's always better to shoot for the moon because even if you miss, you will land among the stars.

Take an example, which of the below options would be more profitable? You set a goal of making $10,000 in a year and reach it... Or...You set a goal of making $500,000 in a year but miss it by a little margin.

Of course, $475,000 is much better than $10,000!

The point here is, even if you miss a bigger goal, it will be much better than obtaining a small goal. The size of your goals will determine the amount of success you would have in your life.

"*The greatest fear for most of us isn't that our aim is too high and we miss it, but that it is too low and we reach it.*" - **Michelangelo,** revered sculptor, painter, architect & poet of the Italian renaissance.

The point here is to go BIG and for something you REALLY want. Set greater goals. Go for the ones which make you feel alive. Only then you will unlock your true potential. Only then you will conjure enough energy to succeed at the highest level. That's how you become the best version of yourself. That's how you become the person you were designed to be.

Don't think of it as work. Your goals should energize you, fill you with positive feelings. If you are in the goal setting process and having a hard time, then something's not right. It should be the most enjoyable step in the whole process.

Get in touch with yourself. Be introspective and find out what you desire the most. It has to be something which means a lot to you.

Some of us are different. Some of us are willing to work much harder if we feel our work will benefit others. Whatever your motivation is (it's your personal choice), just make sure the thought of achieving it makes you happy.

It's important not to limit yourself when setting a goal. Nothing is off-limits in this process. Let it be as wild as it can get. If your craving for your goal is deep enough, it's worth going after. The more intense your desire, the more chance you have of succeeding.

The human brain has evolved over millions of years. There's a world of knowledge and abilities lying in your brain that you are not even aware of. Even if you think a goal is too big for you, that's fine. The only thing required from you at this stage is a well-defined target.

That's it. If you can follow the instructions above and create a goal which excites you, it's a *major* win in itself. I would go as far as to say, selecting the right goal is like being halfway there. It's a big step forward.

Write down your selected goal on a paper. Be as specific as you can about the exact outcome you want. The clearer you are the better.

"Clarity is Power!" - **Anthony Robbins,** Leading motivational speaker & life coach.

Next, set a time limit till when you will accomplish your goals. As mentioned earlier, this part is absolutely vital. It's what turns dreams into reality.

"*The Ultimate inspiration is the deadline.*" - **Nolan Bushnell**, Co-founder of Atari, Inc.

Your time limit is entirely up to your personal preference and the size of your goals. Some people prefer a shorter time frame, while others do well with long term goals. Use your judgment about long it could take to reach there.

As a reminder, don't make the mistake of thinking that you are not yet ready, so it would take a very long time. If this is the first time you are making a serious commitment to a goal, you're going to be greatly surprised at your own abilities when you start taking action.

Have faith that you will certainly achieve your goals. The basic principles for getting achieving any kind of success are the same. No matter what your pursuit is, follow the principles laid out in this book and you will succeed. Thousands of people, just like you, have already achieved success and they have applied the same universal principles you are reading now.

SUMMARY

In a nutshell, keep the following points in mind while setting your goals:

- Make sure the goals you set are really what you desire. Thinking about them should energize you.

- Goals should be extremely clear & well defined. There should be no ambiguity here. Be as detailed as possible.

- Set a date at which you will achieve your goals.

- Write down your goals and their time limit on a physical paper (diary, notebook). Writing down your goals on paper makes them more than just a part of your imagination. Now they exist in the real world.

With this, you have successfully created your goals list. Congrats! You have completed one of the most important steps for achieving success. Make sure you refer to them many times in a day (usually 3-4 times). It should take less than 2 minutes to view them once.

Referring to your goals often will cement them in your mind. Frequent exposure of any kind creates a deep impact on our subconscious brain. It will accept your goals as a target and start looking for ways to reach them.

Chapter #3

PROGRAM YOUR MIND FOR SUCCESS

In this chapter, we'll look into how to develop the mindset of a successful person. No matter how much work you do, without the right mindset, it would be like driving a car with handbrakes on. You would waste a lot of time & energy.

Optimally, you want to have your thoughts supporting you, which will make your journey to success much smoother. In this chapter, we'll cover everything - what beliefs are, why are they important, how to identify negative beliefs and convert them into positive ones.

What are beliefs?

A belief is your sense of certainty about something. That's all. If you are *certain* about what something means, you have a belief about it.

There are two kinds of beliefs: conscious and subconscious. The beliefs which we can *notice* in our mind are conscious beliefs. We are aware of them. If someone asks you to write them down on a piece of paper, you can easily do it. For example, I am a good cook, I can dance well, I am a good person, I help people, etc.

On the other hand, subconscious beliefs are buried deep below our awareness. We cannot articulate them, but we can "feel" their effect. Let's look at an example. Kamal, a friend of mine, was a naturally expressive guy when he was among his friends.

But anytime he found himself surrounded by a few unknown faces (like in a party) he felt "fear".

Now, it's completely normal for people to have little social anxiety, but this was something else. His face would become red and his palms sweaty. He felt threatened and wanted to get out of the situation as fast as possible.

He started taking therapy sessions and, after one year, he discovered the cause of this fear. Actually, when he was a little boy, his family went to attend a large carnival. There were thousands of people at that carnival.

He accidentally got separated from his family and got lost in the crowd. As a little boy, it was a very scary experience. He was getting pushed by oncoming waves of unknown people. Some were looking at him weirdly. Some people tried talking to him which made him even more terrified.

He was later found by the security and taken back to his family. He was fine, but after this fearful experience with unknown people, his subconscious mind formed the belief that "strangers are dangerous".

And he had been carrying this belief deep within his mind ever since, and it really hampered his social life. At the age of 32, he could not articulate *why* he felt fear. He only knew that social situations scared him.

But, after two years of therapy sessions, he was able to uncover the hidden subconscious belief and remove it from his mind. Later, in this chapter, you'll discover ways to find your own limiting subconscious beliefs and how to remove them from your mind.

We all have many conscious and subconscious beliefs about different things in life.

Even now you have beliefs about who you are (as an individual), how other people are and what you deserve out of life. This applies to all areas of your life: relationships, money, business, health, body, mind, etc.

In each of these areas, you have different beliefs that determine how successful you'll be in that particular field. This is true not only for you but for everybody. We all are confined by our beliefs. Research shows the amount of success an individual can have, depends *massively* on where he "believes" his limit to be.

Let's take an example of people who suddenly win the lottery. Maybe they won a million dollars, but somehow they spend all that money and return to the condition they were in before they won the lottery.

This is a powerful example of limiting beliefs in action. These people subconsciously believe they do not deserve to have a million dollars, so they always find a way to spend it and return to their old condition.

"Beliefs create the actual fact." - **William James**, the "Father of American Psychology".

Top experts and coaches of the world like Anthony Robbins & Brian Tracy get you to change your beliefs so that they help you succeed instead of blocking you.

Subconscious & conscious beliefs can be of two types: positive and negative. The beliefs that help you to reach your goals are called positive. For example; I am going to be successful, I am intelligent, I am worthy, and I can do it.

While some beliefs block you from becoming successful. They are called negative (or limiting) beliefs. E.g. I am not good enough, it will not work, I am not qualified enough.

The main purpose of this chapter is to identify and eliminate negative beliefs that are holding us back and install positive, empowering beliefs.

This is critical because our beliefs affect the level of *action* we take. If you have negative beliefs then your mind will come up with hundreds of reasons why you'll never succeed and why it's better to give up right now.

On the other hand, having positive beliefs is like having an internal coach. It will push you to move forward, regardless of the challenges you face.

"We can complain because rose bushes have thorns, or rejoice because thorn bushes have roses." - **Abraham Lincoln**, 16th President of the United States.

Beliefs have a profound effect on your motivation. Positive beliefs grant certainty that you WILL reach your goals, thus providing a big boost to your motivation levels.

Similarly, your motivation is *hindered* by the presence of negative beliefs. A negative belief makes you think all the effort you are applying will eventually go to waste because you'll never reach your goal anyway.

As you can tell, beliefs play a very important part in the process of achieving your goals. It's critical that we get this part of ourselves handled.

How your current beliefs were formed?

Majority of our beliefs were formed during childhood when the brain was learning the ins and outs of the world. And because our childhood environment could be anything, a child's brain forms the beliefs according to the conditions he grew up in.

For example, if a child grows up in a society where there is a lack of money, his brain is likely to form a belief that money is scarce and is something that is very hard to come by. On the other hand, a child who grows up in an abundance of money forms beliefs that money is abundant and easy to come by.

The surprising thing is the randomness of all this. Your negative and positive beliefs are formed based on whatever environment you were in. It is completely random.

But here's the good news, you can change your beliefs at *any* point in your life. When I started out, I had to change many of my negative beliefs and replace them with positive ones. It made a huge difference in the amount of success I had and my overall experience of life.

Let me share a personal experience. When I was in high school, my elder sister gave me a pair of sunglasses. They were very nice and looked good on me. But I didn't wear them to school, because I believed I wasn't "cool enough" to wear them.

Just normal sunglasses.

Such is the powerful effect our beliefs have over us. And the surprising thing is that most of the time we don't even know we have such negative beliefs that are blocking us from achieving what we want.

Beliefs change how we look at the world. They are like lenses from which we look at the world and create its meaning. In presence of positive beliefs, your outlook will be much more optimistic. You will be able to find positives even from a seemingly bad situation.

While negative beliefs will make you focus more on the problems, obstacles, and reasons why you should not even attempt to do something about your situation.

If you pay attention, then you can easily find people around you who have positive beliefs. We all have at least a few people who have a positive outlook on the world. These people are cheerful, optimistic and full of energy.

I highly recommend you stick close to these people as much as possible. Because beliefs, like emotions, are *contagious*. The more time you spend with these people, the more your outlook will change to be positive.

"*You are the average of the five people you spend the most time with.*" - **Jim Rohn**, world-famous motivational speaker, author and entrepreneur.

You will start feeling more energized, enthusiastic and, most importantly, begin believing that you can achieve your dream life.

IMPORTANT: Don't be discouraged if you can't find positive people to hang out with. I discovered that great books, audio, video programs, etc., all count towards changing your mind to be positive. It's not only about the surrounding people. It's about the top five "influences" that affect you on daily basis.

Reading a book by someone who is massively successful *will* influence your mind to think like them. As you continually read, watch or listen to top individuals, you will gradually begin to adopt their beliefs and mindsets, which would be *really* helpful if you can't find people like that in your actual life.

Entitlement

This brings us to another very interesting topic—entitlement. Entitlement is your feeling of "deserving-ness". It determines whether or not you feel deserving of the success you want. This goes for all areas of life—whether you feel deserving of having a great lover in your life, an abundance of money or a completely fit body.

It all depends on your sense of *entitlement*.

Here's another interesting point: entitlement is created by your *beliefs*. For example, if you believe that you are an attractive person, you will feel deserving of having an attractive partner. If you believe that money is hard to come by, you will always struggle with your finances.

Do not confuse entitlement with ego. An egotistical person believes he is *better* than others and automatically deserving of more success. That's narcissism, an unhealthy way of thinking that ultimately leads to downfall.

Entitled people believe that *everybody* has the potential to succeed, and success WILL come if they put in the required effort.

It's all about beliefs...

Every single thing that you do or don't do depends on your feelings of "deserving-ness" and ultimately, your beliefs.

It's essential to get your beliefs in-line with what you want to achieve. This removes all internal resistance and makes the journey to becoming successful much smoother.

How beliefs are created?

Remember our earlier discussion that beliefs are something you are *really* certain about? To get that certainty, we require "evidence" that those beliefs are true. These pieces of evidence are called references.

An example of a reference could be your boss giving you props for completing a report on time. This recognition provides evidence for the belief, "I am competent at my work."

The more references you have, the stronger the belief would be. For example, if a beautiful girl has been getting praise for her beauty since childhood, she will have thousands & thousands of references proving that she is beautiful. Now the belief would be so strong that she doesn't need to even think about it. It is certain in her mind -- she IS beautiful.

Imagine your beliefs like a table-top, and references are the legs of the table. Without legs, the table cannot stand on its own. That's exactly how your beliefs work. References create and hold belief together.

If you remove the legs (or even weaken them), the table-top will fall. Similarly, collecting many pieces of counter-evidence for a belief will weaken it and eventually remove it from your mind.

This is a very powerful understanding. It gives us insight into how our beliefs work and how they can be made stronger or weaker.

If you want to read more about how references shape our beliefs, check out *Awaken the Giant Within* by Anthony Robbins. It's one of my favorite books on the subject of NLP and beliefs.

Now we will use what we have learned to create positive, empowering beliefs, while removing negative beliefs from our mind.

Most Effective Ways To Change Your Beliefs

1. Collect references that reinforce your positive belief

One of the most powerful ways to weaken your limiting beliefs while simultaneously strengthening a positive belief is to *deliberately* collect references for it.

To do this, think about two or three positive beliefs that will benefit you the most. These are the beliefs which you believe will be most helpful to have in your present situation. Now, take a new diary and write these beliefs down on the first page.

This is your table-top or the beliefs you want to have. Now you need to collect references (real-life evidence) to support your selected beliefs.

I would like to share a powerful secret with you. Your subconscious mind (where the beliefs are stored) does not give a damn about reason or logic. It never debates whether something is *rational* or not.

If you provide enough references, it will believe *anything*! You have the potential to have any belief you want in your life.

Now, as you go about your day, keep an eye out for anything which could even *remotely* support your selected beliefs. For example, if one of your selected beliefs is "I am becoming a millionaire", then references to support that belief from your daily life could be:

- I am always on time, just like a millionaire who is punctual. I am going to be one.

- I worked the best I could today, just like the millionaires do. I have what it takes to be a millionaire.

- I have a dream to be a millionaire, and I am working in that direction, just like self-made millionaires did. I am like them. I am going to be one.

This list could be limitless. It only requires creativity and a positive approach. Any small, trivial thing could be your reference. You could even change the meaning of something negative and view it as a reference for your empowering beliefs.

For example, you want to start your own business but are doing a 9-to-5 job to pay your bills. If you are feeling bad about the current situation, you can change its meaning from "this is such a horrible situation. I am stuck here." to "You know what? This horrible experience is the universe's way of forcing me to work harder towards my goal: to create my own business."

You can change the meaning of any situation and view it as a reference to strengthen your empowering beliefs. Many people do it subconsciously... but they do it to reinforce *negative* beliefs such as "people are mean", "money is hard to come by" or "I am not capable".

You will do it consciously... for the positive ones. As you find (or create) references during the day, write them down immediately on your mobile phone so you don't forget them.

When you come home, WRITE THEM DOWN in your diary as "evidence for belief..."

Writing down your thought of paper works like magic. It penetrates deep in your mind. Your collected references will create a deep sense of certainty about your selected belief.

As you continue to collect references for your beliefs, within 4-5 days you will start feeling different. The belief will begin to feel very real.

If you continue to gather references for your empowering beliefs (which you should), they will become so ingrained in your mind that nothing will ever shake them out. You'll have rock-solid beliefs for whole life.

2. Affirmations

Affirmations are positive statements that you repeat again and again to fill your mind with absolute certainty. In our daily life, we are constantly bombarded with countless messages from media like TV, newspapers, and magazines that we are not enough, we'll never be as good as "them", we can't have that, etc.

Do you remember the TV commercial with a young, handsome guy with six-pack abs surrounded by six girls, or a female model with a perfect figure walking down the red carpet, or a celebrity arriving at a hot party in his Lamborghini?

While being completely harmless on the surface, this kind of exposure creates self-doubt in normal men and women about themselves. It subtly creates a "standard" in the minds of people which they believe they could *never* reach.

What this does is lower our confidence in ourselves and our capabilities.

And we need to fight against it. We need to *reclaim* our confidence and self-esteem.

This is where affirmations can help greatly. Affirmations will act as a daily reminder of your capabilities and your value as a person. It will be your daily "boost" of confidence. It will protect your confidence against all sorts of BS thrown at you.

Widely successful people like Oprah Winfrey, Will Smith, Jim Carrey, Arnold Schwarzenegger, and Lady Gaga swear by the effectiveness of affirmations.

Affirmations really do work, but you have to use them correctly. I have been doing affirmations for four years now, and I can honestly say they made a significant positive impact on my life.

How to do affirmations correctly?

1) Write down your doubts and insecurities on a piece of paper. Then, identify five of your *biggest* doubts and insecurities which you believe are holding you back the most.

2) After you have identified five of your biggest doubts, write down their exact opposite positive statement. For example, if your doubts statement is "I don't deserve to be rich", then its opposite positive statement could be "I fully deserve to be rich".

Change all five of your doubts into their opposite positive statements. Write them down on paper.

Note: Make sure all your affirmations are positive and in the present tense. Don't make affirmations for the future, like - I will succeed in the future, I will have a fit body, etc. your mind puts these statements in "maybe in the future" category.

Your affirmations must be positive and in the present tense. Example: I am successful, I deserve to be rich, I have a fit body, I have abundance in my life. Got it? Positive and present tense.

3) Now after you have converted your five negative beliefs into positive ones on paper, write down another five Positive beliefs which you believe will help you the most. These five beliefs are the mindset which you would want to have. For example, I am a good learner, I can deal with any situation, etc.

4) You now have 10 affirmations that you would like to have as beliefs. Five positive ones converted from your negative beliefs, and another five one which you think are great to have. It's time to install these 10 beliefs in your mind. Stand in front of a mirror (preferably full length where you can see your whole body) and look *directly* in your eyes.

5) Say your affirmations out loud. Make sure to say them with PASSION & EMOTION, like you really believe them. You can use your facial expressions and gestures to bring up the emotions while saying your statements. This is very important.

For example, if your affirmation is - I am going to be a millionaire, say it like you *really* mean it! Change your posture. Stand tall, chest forward like you are proud of yourself. Put both of your hands up and shout "YESSSSSSSSS!" in a triumphant voice. FEEL the emotion and passion in your voice.

Now repeat your affirmation two more times.

Do whatever you can to bring emotion into your affirmations. Statements mixed with emotions have a deep penetrating effect on our mind.

Anthony Robbins (success coach, author of *'Unlimited Power'* & *'Awaken The Giant Within'*) and Dr. Joseph Murphy (author of bestselling book *'The Power Of Your Subconscious Mind'*) have also stressed the importance of mixing emotion in your affirmations. Without it, you would be doing affirmations for years without any benefit.

Do your affirmations daily. It only takes about 5 minutes, and within 2-3 weeks you will start noticing changes in your behavior. If you keep doing it, these positive statements will become a permanent part of your mind.

I personally used this technique to change my beliefs and it has worked amazingly well. It only needs a commitment from your part. Don't think about whether it will work or not. Suspend your disbelief and do it for a period of time. When you start noticing the difference, you would never want to stop.

3. Visualization

Visualization is a fancy word for 'vivid imagination' or 'imagined in great detail'.

It's a very effective technique for changing your beliefs. Medical science proved that the human mind cannot differentiate between real life and something vividly imagined.

In an experiment, researchers have placed scanners on the body of an athlete and got him to imagine running on a track in as much detail as possible. Scanners revealed that during visualization, his muscles were activating in the same manner as when doing the actual, physical activity of running on a track.

Since then, multiple researchers have verified the positive effect of visualization on the actual performance of an individual. Now, this fact is widely accepted in sports psychology and trainers put a huge emphasis on regular mental practice along with physical ones.

Now here's the interesting part - we know how beliefs are created and reinforced by 'real-life evidence'. By using visualization, you can provide your subconscious mind any piece of "evidence" you desire because it *cannot* tell the difference between real life and something imagined in detail.

You can vividly imagine a scenario, and your mind will accept it as true. What this essentially means that you can "manufacture" evidence that will reinforce positive beliefs in your mind.

This is a very powerful concept and its possibilities are virtually unlimited. For example, suppose you have social anxiety. You feel nervous about going to a party and talking to people you don't know. If you visualize for 15 minutes that you're in a party full of strangers and are feeling relaxed & calm while socializing with them, your mind will soon accept it as truth and your social anxiety would decrease or entirely disappear.

I personally used visualization to get rid of my fear of public speaking. I had some pretty bad experiences with public speaking. I used to stutter my words, lose my train of thought, wondering what people are thinking about me while standing on stage. It was pretty embarrassing.

But when I found out about visualization and how it works, I decided to give it a try. So, on a night before my big presentation, I closed my eyes and visualized giving a speech in a room full of people.

I felt the same anxiety as when I stand on stage in real life. It was pretty much the same feeling. But, I forced myself to deliver my speech as best as I could. As this was in imagination, whenever I messed up, I stopped & repeat it again and try to do it correctly this time.

It took 15 visualization tries for me to lose almost all of my anxiety while delivering my speech.

The next day, when I actually got on stage, it felt quite familiar. As if I had done it before. I did feel 'some' anxiety but it was quite manageable. My speech went quite well and people came up to me afterward to tell me how clear I was with my message.

Since then, I became a firm believer in the power of visualization. I used visualization in many other areas and it always helped.

Anthony Robbins, Brian Tracy, Jack Canfield, Donald Trump, Napoleon Hill, Zig Ziglar, Dale Carnegie, and countless other extremely successful people firmly stand by the power of visualization.

The best classic books like- *Think and grow rich*, *See you at the top*, *Power of your subconscious mind*, *How to win friends and influence people*, etc - recommend visualization as a tool to reach your goals faster.

On a personal note, the best resource I have found on the topic of visualization is Dr. Maxwell Maltz's book, *Psycho-cybernetics*.

It has helped millions of people change their life for the better. I highly recommend checking it out.

Visualization is a very powerful technique but you have to do it correctly. Follow this simple, step by step method.

How to do visualization correctly?

1- First, sit or lie down in a relaxed, quiet environment. Make sure there are no distractions like excessive noise or lights. You should feel relaxed in this environment. For most people, such a place would be their bedroom.

2- Close your eyes. Take a few deep, relaxed breaths. Consciously relax your body and mind.

3- Once you are feeling relaxed, close your eyes. Start imagining that you have reached your goal. You have achieved what you wanted and now are filled with excitement & joy. Imagine it in as much detail as possible. It should be easy because it's something you really want. You will start feeling really good.

Note: Don't worry. You don't have to do it perfectly. Just add as many details as you can. After little practice, you will be able to visualize in much more detail.

4- Now keep viewing that vision (and feeling good) for few moments (1 to 5 minutes).

5- Open your eyes and relax.

That's it. Visualization is a very simple process (quite relaxing too) but you will find it *amazingly* powerful. You would start feeling like you have almost achieved your desired objective. It will completely change your mindset for the better. You would

feel much more optimistic and motivated. Doubts &
uncertainties would disappear. You would have more focus and
discipline. I wholeheartedly recommend visualization as a
powerful tool to condition yourself for success.

Practice it daily. Preferably, once after getting up in the morning
and once before sleep at night. It takes only 5-10 minutes and is
very effective for obtaining success in ANY area of life.

Now, it's up to you.

We have covered beliefs and their significance. We also covered
three effective ways to develop positive, empowering beliefs.
Make frequent to use these tools. You will find them very useful
for achieving your desired outcome.

Chapter #4

TURNING DREAMS INTO REALITY

One of the essential aspects of obtaining success is being well prepared. You should know exactly what you want and how you will go about getting it. This does not necessarily mean that you must have a complete and concrete plan at the start of your journey. If you do have a clear plan, great! But more often, people starting their journey don't have any idea how they will achieve their goals.

They simply know what they want—and that's the most important part.

After studying countless stories of successful people, it became clear to me that not a single one of these people followed a clearly defined path to their goals. No one knew exactly how they would succeed in the future.

What they had was a clear vision of the goal.

Next critical step is planning, which makes achieving success easier. But before we continue, here's a quick refresher about planning.

Let's take a look...

Planning defined

Oxford defined planning as "a detailed map or a diagram".

Overall, planning is the process of setting goals, developing strategies, outlining tasks, scheduling activities, establishing procedures, setting a time limit, and managing roles.

Phew!

In simpler words, planning is deciding in advance what is to be done, when & where it is to be done, how it is to be done and by whom.

It's a road map of activities which need to be done so you move towards your goals.

This single idea - planning - is the reason your dreams become your reality. It converts an idea in your mind to something real... something which can be done in the present moment to ACTUALLY move towards what you want.

For example, Joe gets the idea that he should start his own business. He likes the thought of being an entrepreneur and feels excited. He thinks he would certainly start working on his business... soon.

He keeps this thought in his mind and gets caught up in his daily routine and responsibilities. The thought and the excitement of being an entrepreneur soon start fading away. And whenever the thoughts of starting his own business come in his mind, he justifies "oh, but I don't have enough time. I will do it later"

And that time never comes...

I have seen countless times people get an insight, an idea about what they should do, and they let that idea fade away. It's very disheartening. I personally have been in this place myself (many times actually) so I know exactly how it feels.

But let's take another example, this time Joe gets it right. He does not let the idea fade away.

First, he writes down the thought on a piece of paper (or a mobile notepad). When he gets home after work, he opens a diary and writes down that idea on top of the page.

Then he starts thinking about every possible activity or person which could help him move in the direction in his goals... Read "how to start a business" books, attend seminars on building a business, get his friend's entrepreneur contact to give advice on what he should do to create his product, and so on.

(Always remember: nobody at the start of their journey knew EXACTLY how they will reach their goals and this is not important at first. The most important thing at the beginning is to DECIDE what is it that you want and trust that you will reach your goals. That is the most important part. This fact will be repeated several times again in upcoming chapters because it is so important to remember but so easy to forget.)

Joe makes a list of these and starts doing them one by one regularly. Each one of these activities moves Joe one step closer to his goal. Every activity leads to new insights and soon he gets a clear vision of the path that he has to take. Eventually, Joe starts his business on small scale and its expansion becomes his new goal.

With time and persistence, Joe will eventually succeed.

Joe was able to start his business because he did not let the thought fade away, by doing something about it. He wrote down his goal on paper. He thought about activities and people which could help. He made a list.

This is called planning. It does not have to be very thorough and scientifically precise. Any simple plan would do. As you gain experience by working on it, you would make changes in your plan to make it better and better.

This is how every successful person started their journey. Never believe even for a second that "high achievers" had a clear cut plan to their goal from the very beginning. It never works that way.

"*I try to learn from the past, but I plan for the future by focusing exclusively on the present. That's where the fun is.*" - **Donald Trump**, 45th and current president of the United States (2019), businessman and television personality.

Successful people decide on a goal and start with whatever they know. No matter how trivial the knowledge is.

It is never about the perfect start because there IS no perfect start.

Success comes from going with whatever minor lead you have at the start and as you gain experience and perspective, you make changes in your approach... And you keep moving forward until you reach your goal.

That is what creates success.

How to make effective plans?

Now that we have covered why planning is such an indispensable part of success, let's take look at some strategies that will help you formulate the best possible plan with whatever information you have got. Keep in mind, these strategies are universal in nature. They can be used to create effective plans in any field.

1. Collect information

To be able to create any kind of plan, you need information first. Fortunately, today you have more information available to you than ever before. In fact, there is more information available than you need.

So it's much better to sort and take information which you require. Otherwise, you will be constantly absorbing information and end up wasting your time.

But how will you know which Information to take out and which to ignore?

My answer is to look at your goal. What do you need to accomplish? What you have to currently do? What "current issues" you need to handle? What do you need to do "this" moment?

Asking yourself these questions will clarify your thoughts, and make you focus on selecting ONLY that information which you need to sort out your current problem and move you forward.

Some people might say "but I also collect information which could benefit me in the future". Don't fall for this trap. There are two reasons for which you would not want to do that.

First, you will be overwhelmed by the amount of information you would collect. Let me ask you a question. Is there any information that has no value to you?

No. All information could benefit you in one way or the other. So if you get into the mindset that you are collecting information that has the "potential" to help you, you will end up collecting a LOT of info. It will overwhelm you and pull you off track.

This will result in the second problem. You will waste a lot of time. Because there is a virtually unlimited amount of information available right now, you will get confused over it and end up wasting valuable time, which could have been spent actually taking action.

Always remember: information is valuable ONLY if it allows to take RIGHT ACTION. You must have heard that old saying- "*knowledge is not power, it the application of knowledge that creates power.*"

If you are only collecting a lot of information but not doing anything about it, you are wasting your time. Knowledge without its application is of no use. Don't make this mistake.

Process of collecting information - step by step:

a) Think about your goal. What do you need to accomplish ultimately? For example, your goal is to make a million dollars, or be more loving to your partner, or have a fit body with 7% body fat, etc.

b) Think about what do you need to do NOW to move towards your ultimate goal? What is the next step to your destination? Figure it out. Be very clear. For example, to create million dollars from your business, you need to learn how to expand your business, or if your goal is to find an attractive partner, your current step could be to go to social events.

If in case you don't know what your current step is, or how to move forward from your present situation... That is what you currently need. You need to figure out what your "current step" should be.

c) Now you can search for the RELEVANT information which would help you with your present need. Information should be clear and should be enough to get you past your current stage. For example, if you need to go to social events to find an attractive mate, you must search for the information on the current social event in your area.

Be warned, when you start searching for social events, you are bound to come across information like "how to attract a partner" or "how to become more attractive". These kinds of information are very valuable, no doubt. But it is not something you require now.

Don't fall into the trap of "over-collecting" information and venture off the path. Just select the required information for your current step and take ACTION on it. For the earlier example, go to the social event. Start interacting with people. If after some time, you don't seem to get the attention of the opposite sex, then that becomes your current step.

Now you should search and collect information on "how to be attractive". This will make you much more efficient as well as effective. You will charge through your path to your goal. People, who make the mistake of over-collecting information, lose their focus and delay taking action, losing a lot of precious time in the process.

It also lowers their motivation. They feel anxiety that there is just so much to learn. They will not be able to learn it all, therefore not succeed.

2. Create a blueprint plan

Next, what you should do, is to create a blueprint plan. Actually, it's nothing but an outline of the actual steps you would take. You collect all the information and condense it down to simple, easy to follow action steps.

It is miles better than what many people do - having no plan at all. Please don't do this. Create a general frame of what you should do.

I am calling it 'general' because it's a fresh and tentative plan which should help you get started initially, and later on, as you gain more experience and information, you should make changes in it accordingly.

Here is an example of a blueprint plan.

Suppose your goal is to lose your belly fat and get in shape. Your blueprint plan could be -

1st step - Join a gym

2nd step - Get familiar with exercises (hire a trainer if needed)

3rd step - Start working out 5 times a week (or as needed)

4th step - Gain information about what to eat and what to avoid

5th step - Start eating healthy

6th step - Keep improving your workout and diet

And so on...

Another example:

If you want to expand your online business:

1st step - Read four marketing books this month

2nd step - Understand your niche better (study competitors, do a survey, etc)

3rd step - Contact and set up meetings with your marketing people

4th step - Try three different marketing strategies in the next two months

And so on...

Having a blueprint plan will give you something concrete to follow up with. It will allow your ideas to take shape in the real world.

And the best part is - it can be updated as you gain more ideas and experience. The flexibility to grow is a major strength of a blueprint plan. Never wait for the 'perfect plan'. There will never be a perfect plan at the start.

You have to get clear about your goal and create a blueprint plan with whatever information you currently have. Most successful people started with whatever information they had and made corrections along the way.

Bill Gates and Microsoft

Bill Gates had the vision to open a software business, but different situations & challenges made him go through several different phases. His first company TRAF-O-DATA came to an end. He joined college but did not find it to his interest. He joined Honeywell, but his close friend Allen kept pushing him to open a new software company. Within a year, Bill Gates dropped out of college and co-founded Microsoft with Paul Allen.

3. Break it down

If you have a big task included in your plan, and it feels daunting... it is much better to break it down into smaller parts.

For examples, suppose you have a goal of getting into shape. It can be very confusing to know how to go about it. In this case, you have to break it down into smaller, more manageable parts. Find out your protein requirement and have it every day. Add greens like kale, spinach, broccoli & clean meats like chicken to your intake. Drink 2-3 liters of waters each day.

"Getting into shape" is a pretty broad term in itself. It does not convey what exactly needs to be done. Breaking It into smaller parts will allow you to know exactly but you need to do and when. It increases the effectiveness of your plan several folds.

4. Add a deadline

It's very important to include dates in your plan. Having a deadline will do several positive things-

> a) It will put positive pressure on you to take action, making sure you are not taking things too casually or acting lazy. It will make you much more efficient.

b) A deadline will allow you to measure your progress. For example, suppose you are writing your book and your plan is to finish 2 chapters in 15 days (deadline). if you have not been able to complete your first chapter for 8 days, it will become clear that your progress is slow. You will be forced to check where you are slipping and what you should do to get back on track.

c) It will make your goals feel real and subsequently increase your motivation. For example- If your goal is to buy a new car, Toyota Camry, which of the following plans feel more real and motivating--

    1) I will buy a Toyota Camry...

    2) I will buy Toyota Camry within next six months.

Quite a difference, right? Be sure to add a deadline in front of your goals.

Obstacles in planning

Till now, we covered why planning is important and how to make effective plans. Now let's discuss some of the major roadblocks people face while planning and how to get past them. These are two of the most common problems I have seen people deal with during the planning stage.

1. Procrastination

The first roadblock is procrastination. People make excuses. They delay creating their plans, and come up with various reasons why they would create a plan "later". There could be several excuses- "I don't have time", "I don't have enough resources", "I have never done something like this before", "the economy is bad", "I have to do this others thing first" and the most common one- "I will do it later.."

Procrastination can slow down your progress and can keep you away from creating your blueprint plan. The best way to counter procrastination is to find out why do you want to achieve this goal? Why do you want what you want?

State all the possible reasons for wanting to achieve this goal. How will it benefit you? How will it benefit people around you and your society?

Figuring out your "why" is very, very effective for moving past procrastination. Excuses come up only when you lose your emotional drive for your goals. It is directly linked to your level of motivation. (Note: If you want to learn more about motivation, check out chapter 6.)

Here, figuring out your "why" and reviewing it every day will be very effective for pushing past procrastination. Here is what you should do:

1) Make a list of all the reasons why you want to achieve your goals.

2) Review this list twice a day: every morning when you get up & before sleeping at night. It should not take more than 3 - 4 minutes.

3) Lastly, imagine that you have achieved your goals and feel good as if every single reason on your list came true. Imagine how it would feel.

If you do this simple exercise of around 3 minutes (depending on how long your list is) you will completely eliminate procrastination and excuse making. You will be unstoppable!

"Find your WHY and you'll find your WAY" - **John C. Maxwell**, American author, speaker and pastor.

2. Lack of belief in your abilities

The second most common problem people face while planning for their success is the lack of belief in themselves and their abilities. Most people have not-so-encouraging past (to put it mildly) and currently are in a situation where they are constantly reminded that they cannot do anything right.

For example - In your job, your boss may tell you time-to-time that you made a mistake in the submitted report, or you say something and your colleague 'corrects' you. It can also happen in family, neighborhood, friends, etc.

All of these instances may seem little and insignificant, but they gradually weaken your self-confidence. If you are constantly reminded of your mistakes and fumbles, your mind would start doubting your abilities. This gives birth to 'lack of self-belief'.

Two things will help you out here -

a) Everybody Makes Mistakes

First, realize that even the most successful people in the world make mistakes regularly. They make wrong decisions, give politically incorrect statements in public, forget something important, etc. Nobody is perfect. Let's look at some examples.

1. Anthony Robbins once made a mistake in judging the quality of management of his company, which resulted in a debt of $750,000.

2. Michael Jordon missed more than 9000 shots in his career, lost almost 300 games, missed game-winning shot 26 times, but still considered the greatest basketball player in history.

Everyone makes mistakes. It's all right. It is very human to make mistakes. Never beat yourself down because you made a mistake. Everyone fumbles everyday one way or the other. What separates the best from the rest is - successful people believe the mistakes are inevitable, and the ONLY thing we can do after making a mistake is to LEARN from it.

Find out why you made the mistake, how did it happen, what caused it and what you will do in the future to avoid it as best as you can.

That's it!

Once you have taken the lessons out of it, forget that you ever made the mistake. It is non-existent for you. People keep on beating themselves over their mistake for days. Don't do that. Just let it go. Mistakes serve no useful purpose after you have learned your lesson. Forget about it. Focus your attention on the present moment.

b) Reinforce positive beliefs

Second, you need to create and reinforce in your mind that you are fully capable of achieving your goals. This is even more important if your current environment is constantly forcing you to believe that success is not possible and it's beyond your abilities.

If you don't 'actively' reinforce self-belief on daily basis, then it is very natural to succumb to your environment and lose faith in yourself. The previous chapter on beliefs was all about what we are discussing here. If you need more self-belief & confidence in yourself & your capability, go and re-read that chapter. It will help you out greatly.

Chapter #5

FASTEST LANE TO SUCCESS

"There is no substitute for hard work. Always be humble and hungry." - **Dwayne 'The Rock' Johnson**, premier Hollywood star.

Nothing ever can be achieved without putting in hard work. Most people do not put enough emphasis on taking action. It is 'THE' most important part of achieving success.

If you do nothing else but select a goal and start working toward it, you will eventually achieve it. On the other hand, even if you follow all the suggestions outlined in this book, if you don't take necessary action on your part, you will not get anywhere.

The rest of the principles of success are there to make your journey easier, but nothing can replace hard work. It carries significance and will open an additional door to your destination as you put in the required efforts.

I firmly believe that even if you don't have a plan when you begin, if you continue to take action, you will find a way.

As mentioned in Chapter 3, the human brain is extremely capable of finding solutions. It has the ability to find data that is not visible at the surface. This biological phenomenon is thoroughly covered in books - *Psycho-cybernetics* by Maxwell Maltz and *The power of your subconscious mind* by Joseph Murphy. These books have helped people all over the world change their lives for the better.

Anytime you work towards a selected goal, your subconscious mind starts looking for the most efficient way to reach it. It's an amazing goal-seeking system. It actively looks for the fastest, shortest, most effective route to your goal. Your mind learns from the mistakes and corrects its path.

You have so many amazing tools at your disposal that you don't even know yet. As you go further in this book, we will uncover many such traits of human beings which will allow you to achieve anything you desire.

The only prerequisite is your commitment to hard work. While you are blessed with amazing abilities, you still have to USE them.

Let's take visualization, for example. It's extremely effective in changing your behavior, beliefs, motivation. But it will not work without putting in effort from your side.

Taking action is the single most important piece in solving the puzzle of success. Many people read different books, surf the internet, attend seminars, get professional help and eventually formulate a step-by-step plan. But they do not take enough action to make everything come together & create success.

Hard work brings certainty

Hard work will provide more certainty of success than any other knowledge or education. Let's look at an example. Alex was a newly appointed salesman. He had no prior sales experience or training. But he had a special ability—he was a hard worker. Although his start was rough, within two years he shot ahead of his peers who were more experienced than him.

I asked him about his secret to success. His answer was "It was simple! Other people were making thirty cold calls a day and I was making ninety. Other were visiting five or six clients a day, I was visiting more than twelve."

He continued, "Even though I didn't completely believe that I could become number one sales guy because I was far behind in experience than my colleagues. But doing three times more work made me learn three times faster, as well. I began believing in myself and it changed everything."

Experience is the best teacher, and it can only come from hard work.

"*A dream doesn't become reality through magic. It takes sweat, determination and hard work*." - **Colin Powell**, former United States national security advisor.

Never compare yourself with others

One thing important thing to remember when you are doing this is to not look at other people. Walk on your own path. You will see people who achieved success easily and begin to doubt yourself. Don't do that. Everyone is on their own journey in life.

Human tendency is to look at other people and compare them with ourselves. "Am I doing better than Sam? Am I doing worse than Suzy?"

It's one of the most common mistakes we make and something which you must avoid completely. These comparisons distract you. When you make the performance of others your benchmark, you will never reach your own personal best.

The only way to uncover your true potential is to focus on improving yourself and your own performance as much as possible. The only benchmark you have to beat is your current personal best. That's it.

Don't let any compliments boost your ego, or any criticisms shake your confidence. Do your personal best at the moment and look for ways to improve it next time. Always.

Action breeds success: Will Smith

Will Smith, the Hollywood heartthrob, attributes his success to his work ethic. His famous quote, "You might have more talent than me, you might be smarter than me, you might be attractive than me, you can beat me in everything, but when we get up on a treadmill two things may happen. Either you get off first or I will die at the treadmill. I will not be outworked!"

How to take massive action and be unstoppable?

Now we get to the core of this chapter - how to take action the right way and let nothing stop on your track.

1. Align your lifestyle with your goals

First, you will have to build a foundation for doing hard work. Taking action requires a lot of energy, concentration, time, effort, and discipline. It's not easy.

(It's called HARD WORK after all)

To do it successfully over long periods of time, you'll need to change your lifestyle into something which supports you. The way we normally spend our daily life, determines our energy level, discipline, mood, and willpower significantly.

For example, if you eat food containing lots of sugar at breakfast, you will have an energy crash mid-morning and struggle with energy for the rest of day.

Sugar gives an instant burst of energy, but soon your energy drops to an even lower level than before. (Search online for the effects of sugar on your energy and mood.)

Similarly, frequent late nights, drinking lots of alcohol, eating processed foods— all take a toll on your mind and body, making you less energetic and dulling your concentration.

You must take control over your lifestyle, so that you feel alive, energetic, positive, and raring to go!

A good lifestyle means the following:

• Good nutrition

• Quality & quantity of sleep

• Exercise

• Your peers. Surround yourself with positive, upbeat people.

• Read books and success stories

• Cut down negative influences like TV, magazines, toxic people, etc.

Get this part of your daily life in order. When you do this, you will feel great most of the time. You will have a balanced mental and physical condition to exert a lot of effort.

2. Plan your mood and energy levels in advance

Some people have more energy in the morning, while others do their best work at night. Whatever your preferred time to work is, you need to schedule your day so that the majority of your most important work falls on the time of the day when you perform your best.

For example, I am a morning person. I tend to do my best in the morning. I can also work in the afternoon and night, but the quality & quantity of my morning work is far superior.

The same thing goes for your energy levels. Our energy levels tend to fluctuate during the course of the day. Some people feel more energetic in the morning and others during the day or late at night... Plan your day around it.

Try working at different times of the day to find your own preferred time period in which you feel most energetic, and schedule your work at that time.

This simple step will increase the quality and quantity of your work tremendously. As stated earlier, when you take care of your health, mood, influences, etc., you will feel energetic most of the time during the day. In other words, your "peak performance time" window will get bigger.

When you plan your activity in "peak performance" time (which has increased), you would do your best work for long periods of time.

3. What to do if your work seems overwhelming?

It's easy to get overwhelmed by seeing how much work we have to do. We start doubting whether we can ever finish the work required to achieve the goal.

This kind of thought reduces our motivation, and we subconsciously began to delay the actions we need to take. This was a HUGE problem I faced every time I went after a big goal. I found it's not only me, but everyone is facing the same problem.

After much trial and error, I found the most effective solution for this problem.

Focus on doing your 'current task' as best as you can, and have faith that you did the best possible thing you could do for obtaining your goal in the future.

That's it! Just fully concentrate on your current action and do it in the best way possible. Don't think about the future goal, as it will distract you from your current task. Doing your best work now is the biggest step you can take towards your goal.

Leave the rest to faith. You did your part in the best way possible.

Now, sometimes you will feel overwhelmed again when you think about how much more you have to do. You will begin to question yourself—"Is worth it?","Am I doing it right?","Will success come?","Is my work good enough?"

It can be very scary and disheartening. But knowing the fact that doing your current task with 100% effectiveness is the best possible thing you can do, and it's the ONLY variable you can control. No one else could have done anything more. Even the most successful and richest people struggle with this from time to time.

That's the most anyone can do. So, be proud of yourself. You took the biggest possible step towards your goal.

Combine this with belief strengthening exercises mentioned in Chapter 3: Beliefs, to reinforce the belief that you WILL reach your goal.

100% belief that you will succeed + Do your best at the current task = Massive Success!

"Don't stop when you are tired. Stop when you are done." - **Marilyn Monroe**, famous American actress, model and singer.

4. Plan your week, month and year

The next step is to plan your activity and focus for the entire next week, month and possibly year. Decide the number of hours you will spend working, and fit time for it in your day.

Additional tip: Try to plan your work at the time when you feel most energetic and focused.

People, who don't fit time for this activity, keep on delaying the work hour after hour and end up doing little to no work done. Do the opposite. Schedule time in which you will take action daily. This will help you avoid procrastination. You will not delay work because it is scheduled. Either you do it or you don't.

There is no chance of "I will do it later syndrome," which is one of the most common obstacles people face when doing work.

Conclusion: Schedule time for your activity. It makes a big difference in the long term.

5. Follow through even if you are not in the mood

After you schedule time for working, follow through no matter what. Always do your best. It takes discipline from you. No matter how you are feeling, no matter what excuse you mind is giving you—"Just leave it," "I am not in the mood," "I just want to see this episode on TV," "My friends are going out. I want to go too."

Ignore everything and just start doing your work. If you are REALLY not in the mood to do your work, you will have a 'bad' start. But instead of stopping, keep working. Initially, your mind will resist, but don't stop.

After a little while, your mind will stop resisting the work and accept the fact that work HAS to be done. Then you will be able to work with full effectiveness.

6. Cultivating willpower and discipline

Sometimes 'pushing yourself' is not enough. Maybe you just can't push yourself that much. In that case, you need more willpower to push yourself through excuses & bad emotions and do the work.

Some people say discipline is more important. I beg to differ. I believe if you have enough willpower you will be able to maintain a disciplined life easily. Think of willpower as fuel for discipline. You won't be able to maintain discipline if your willpower is lacking.

In her excellent book *Maximum Willpower*, Kelly McGonigal says willpower is like a muscle. It gets exhausted with use. The more discipline or willpower requiring activities we do, our willpower reserves keeps on reducing.

If it reaches a very low level, then it will be very difficult to fight with excuse making and procrastination. Thankfully, there are ways to recharge and even strengthen your willpower reserve.

The easiest and the most effective way to increase your will power is to meditate for 10-15 minutes daily.

I believe this rare exercise is a MUST for everyone who aspires for success. Do meditation daily and within two months, you will start noticing increased willpower and countless other benefits like - increased calmness, emotional balance, concentration, focus, happiness, and reduced stress & negative thoughts.

Once you start seeing its benefits, you would be surprised why someone didn't tell you about it earlier.

Now before we start, let me tell you that the core practice of meditation had no attachment with any religion. At it very core, the meditation is about focusing on your breath for a short period of time. We are not concerned with spirituality here.

While meditation can be a powerful spiritual practice, you always have an option of not attaching it with any religion and still get the practical, daily life benefits of increased will power and discipline.

It's very easy to do and take only 10 to 15 minutes a day to get the full benefits.

How to meditate?

a) Set an alarm for 15 minutes.

b) Sit comfortably on a chair, keeping your back relaxed & upright. Use Cushion if you need to.

c) Close your eyes and start noticing your breath coming in and out. Notice everything about it: when it enters in your nostrils to when it goes in your diaphragm. The movement of your stomach going up and down, etc.

d) Eventually, your mind will start thinking about something. You will get lost in your thoughts. You lose focus on your breath and start dwelling on the thought itself. It's Ok.

e) Whenever you catch yourself focusing on your thoughts instead of being aware of your breath, gently and calmly shift your focus to your breath.

f) Soon you will lose your focus again and get lost in thoughts. Relax & simply shift your focus to your breath calmly.

g) Keep doing this for 15 minutes till your alarm rings.

Note: Don't force yourself to keep your mind empty all the time. The mind will think and that's what we want. Actually, willpower gets stronger when you keep shifting your focus from your thoughts to your breath. This two-and-forth of awareness is what strengthens willpower muscles. It's like a gym for your mind.

This simple exercise will increase your willpower levels to astronomical levels. Its effectiveness is unmatched. I would even confess that I would not be able to finish this book if it wasn't for meditation. In our society, our daily life has become so demanding that we end up having a very low reserve of willpower.

This simple exercise is the answer. It will replenish the lost supply of willpower and even increase its capacity. Highly, highly recommended.

7. Discomfort is temporary

When you are following through and making a constant effort, you will feel periods of discomfort or even pain. But you'll have to preserve. The discomfort is temporary. It may feel bad right now, but the eventual result will be well worth it!

But it's not all about the result. Time and time again, after people achieve their goal, they value the hardship, the effort they made more than the actual outcome itself.

"True happiness is never the goal which you achieve, but the journey and the person you become who is able to achieve that goal." **- Old proverb**

Think of it as purification of self. It's a rite of passage you have to go through to achieve your desire. The pain and discomfort might be here right now and you hate it as much as possible, but later it will be the part which makes you the proudest.

I still remember a time when success literature was just a hobby of mine; I wanted a new corporate job with better pay. I was not looking for a small salary hike, I wanted to double my current pay. It was a big goal, and trust me, it led to some pretty rough time in the interviews.

As soon as the interviewers found that I want twice the salary, they said NO immediately, thinking I was either greedy or arrogant. Some wanted to know the reason behind it, but after hearing my answer they would generally say no.

Some laughed at me, some told me to leave immediately, but I kept it up. I knew I would find someone who will accept it. I kept doing interviews, kept trying different approaches. Finally, one interviewer said 'OK'. There was an emergency vacancy they wanted to fill as soon as possible and I fit the bill pretty well, in spite of higher pay.

Luck? I don't think it was luck. If I didn't have the courage to keep going and giving interviews, I would never have landed opportunity like that.

Action creates luck. The more action you take, the luckier you become.

And after all these years, if you ask me what I really cherish about that memory, my answer would be - my willingness to push forward even in the face of discomfort and rejection.

That feat is much more valuable for me than getting a bigger paycheck. Experiences like that shape the character of a person and subsequently, his destiny.

True happiness is never the goals you achieve. It's always the person you BECOME during the process.

Work hard and do your best. What seems like pain or discomfort right now will become your most cherished memory later.

Chapter #6

KEEP THE FIRE BURNING

"Obstacles are the cost of greatness." - **Robin Sharma**, famous author and success coach.

Have you ever found yourself NOT doing the work that you KNOW you should do? Do you remember the last time you thought "Oh, I will do it later"? or had thoughts like "I know I should do that, but... (insert your favorite excuse here)"?

If the answer is 'yes' to any of the above questions then you lack the motivation required to take action. In this chapter, we will cover motivation in detail and several effective ways to raise your motivation level.

Let's dive right in...

Motivation is an emotion

Motivation is a special kind of emotion. It's a drive or desire to do something. It pushes us to take action and move towards a specific outcome. Because of this, motivation is crucial for the attainment of any worthwhile goal.

While healthy levels of motivation pump you up to take action, lack of the same can make you lazy and stagnant.

The more motivated you are, the more compelling taking action becomes. The lesser your motivation level, the more you are likely to procrastinate and make excuses. You can call motivation as the archrival of procrastination and laziness. In presence of high enough motivation, the individual will ignore any excuse and do what's required.

Successful people all over the world realize the power of motivation. They invest a lot of time, effort and money to maintain high levels of motivation.

My experience with motivation

Taking action is an important part of achieving success, and also one of the most difficult. We have to deal with criticism, excuses, rejections, failures, bad habits, lack of energy, social influence...

The list goes on & on...

It can be a daunting task if you lack the motivational power. In turn, it's easier to get past all the excuses and hurdles when you feel motivated to do something. Motivation will push you across every obstacle on your path.

Here's a personal example of how increased motivation can drive us to make bigger efforts every day.

In the summer of 2011, I needed to change my apartment. It was in bad shape, and the rent had increased significantly in recent months. Living there was uncomfortable, but not to an extent that would force me to do something about it on an urgent basis.

Even though thoughts about changing my apartment frequently invaded my mind, I did nothing about it and kept living there with 'slight discomfort'.

Then, a major change happened.

The owner of my apartment decided to begin re-construction work. Suddenly many people were hammering at the walls and water pipes. Dust and debris were everywhere (to which I am allergic) and the worst part was that the water supply was hampered because of the ongoing construction work in the entire building.

All of a sudden, it became much more uncomfortable to live there. Changing the apartment became my first priority. Earlier I used to ignore the thoughts of searching a new place to live, and now it became my prime goal.

My motivation was soaring. I immediately started visiting new apartments and did not stop until I found a new place to move in.

The way motivation DIRECTED my attention on a single goal, and kept it there, made me realize how powerful motivation can be. From that point, my search for a deeper understanding of the subject began.

A blessing in disguise

Motivation is a blessing. If you are motivated to do something great, consider yourself 'blessed'.

Very few people are blessed with the motivation to make things better. If you have the compulsion to create a better future for yourself and society, you are extremely fortunate. Don't take your motivation lightly. You are one in a thousand individuals who have the desire to change.

Do yourself and society a favor and capitalize on it. It will not be there forever. With time, everything either weakens or becomes stronger. Use your motivation to your advantage.

Keep increasing it using the methods given later in this chapter, and create a better future for you and for everyone.

A divine spark

I firmly believe that all the success in the world comes from a little thought in your mind: "Hey, I must do something about it."

Bill Gates motivation

A real-life example would be the creation of Microsoft. The multi-billion-dollar business we now know as Microsoft came from an idea in the mind of a young boy named Bill Gates. He had a vision of a personal computer on every desk and in every home, running Microsoft software. His idea of accessible personal computers revolutionized the whole world.

Sometimes, many of us get great ideas, but 99.99 percent of us don't do anything about them. If we followed through, the world would become a better place than even our wildest imaginations.

How to increase your motivation?

Now we come to the core of this chapter- how to increase motivation and sustain it at high levels. The techniques for increasing motivation mentioned below are among the most effective ones that I have found after trying out everything under the sun for more than 13 long years.

I have tried them all - from NLP and punishment/reward to visualization and energy works such as EFT, and these are some of the best ones I ever came across.

1. "Why": Your Core Reasons

"When you find your why, you find a way to make it happen." - **Eric Thomas**, motivational speaker and author.

The first very effective method is to make a list about WHY you want to achieve your goals. What are the reasons for which you crave your desire? How will the realization of your goals help you and others? What will it allow you to do or feel? What positive changes will it bring?

These are the reasons for which you want to acquire your goals.

And your reasons can be of any kind - financial, physical, spiritual, mental. Whatever they may be, if they make you 'feel' even slightly motivated, add them to your list. Make sure your reasons are authentic, which means they are your own personal reasons. Whenever you think about them, you feel excited. The higher the number of reasons in your list, the better.

More than any individual reason, it's the cumulative impact of this list which will boost your motivation to a much higher level. And best of all, it is available to you all the time. You can view this list at any moment you need.

Now some people ask why this has to be a 'written' list. Why can't they just have these in mind?

My answer is: writing down these reasons is very powerful. There has been a lot of research done about the positive impact of the written word. Whenever we write something down, it affects our subconscious mind at a very deep level. Additionally, you can view this list anytime you need a boost in your motivation.

Another important point is to make sure your reasons are positive, not negative. For example, "I will be fully financially independent when I achieve my goal" is a positive reason. Don't write it as "I will be able to pay my bills and move out of this horrible situation".

See? The first reason is written in a positive tone and feels much more uplifting and powerful. The second makes you focus on the negative, even if its overall meaning is positive.

"*Life is about focusing on what you want, not on what you don't want*" **- Anthony Robbins,** life coach and entrepreneur.

So make sure your reasons are written in a positive tone, which will make you focus on the positive effects of achieving your goals.

In a nutshell:

   • Make a list of positive, empowering reasons for you want to achieve your goals. Make sure you select reasons which make you FEEL pumped up.

   • Write it down on a piece of paper.

   • Review this "why" list, at least three times in a day, preferably once in the morning after waking up and two more times later in the day.

2. Meditation

The human mind is beautifully imperfect. Sometimes, even pumped-up emotions are not enough to make you take action. Sometimes the urge to postpone work overcomes even the strongest of motivation.

You know you should go and do what needs to be done, but you make excuses. You procrastinate. You resist taking action.

And motivation doesn't seem to work.

What you need here is WILLPOWER to take action even if you are not in the mood to do it and the DISCIPLINE to not let yourself get distracted by other things. Both willpower and discipline are very powerful traits by themselves, and their effectiveness multiplies several-fold if you incorporate both in your behavior.

You might say, "That's great, Vishal! But how the heck I am supposed to develop willpower AND discipline?"

The answer is meditation. Just 10-15 minutes of daily meditation works like MAGIC in developing willpower and discipline.

There is a whole array of scientific research on meditation and its effects.

In her excellent book *'Maximum Willpower'*, Kelly McGonigal says we have a finite reserve of willpower and discipline. The more you tap into these reserves, the faster they would get drained. Meditation is an actual practice which replenishes these reserves and can even expand them.

Medical research has shown meditation activates and develops the pre-frontal cortex part of our mind which is known to be the command center of behavioral traits like willpower.

In my own personal experience, I have found meditation to be the best and the most effective way to develop willpower and discipline. It's even more effective than taking medical drugs or stimulants for cultivating these two traits.

And as an added bonus, you will experience many other useful benefits - increased concentration, calmness, relaxation, and happiness, to name a few.

If you read about the most successful people, celebrities, athletes - who are at the top of their chosen field - all practice and recommend meditation. Katy Perry, Madonna, Hugh Jackman, Oprah Winfrey, Bill Ford, Kobe Bryant, Russell Simmons, and Anthony Robbins all praise meditation as one of the biggest factors in their success.

If you are trying to become successful or going after any goal you want, add 15 minutes of meditation in your day. It is so effective that once you start seeing the benefits, you would never want to stop.

If you have never done meditation before, I have some good news. The practice of meditation is very simple and you won't have to dwell on any religious aspects that people associate with meditation.

At its core, meditation is simply a practice of focusing on your breath. That's it. None of the religious associations are necessary for meditation.

For an easy step-by-step guide to meditation, check out the "meditation" part of the previous chapter on hard work.

Just follow the simple instructions and start doing meditation daily. You will be surprised by the effect on your discipline and willpower level. As a result, you will overcome excuses and take a lot more action.

And when the discipline and willpower from meditation are used in conjunction with reviewing your "why" list regularly, you will be unstoppable. You will be able to overcome any excuse, any resistance, any feeling which stops you from taking the required action.

3. Visualization

Visualizing your goal is also a very effective way to increase motivation. As we discussed earlier in Chapter 3, the human mind cannot tell the difference between reality and detailed imagination.

Regular practice of visualization exposes your mind to your goals vividly. This detailed exposure makes your subconscious mind accept your goals as a target and makes your RAS (reticular activating system) focus on achieving it.

You will feel an increased 'urge' to go for your goals. It's not a logical thought. It's a feeling. And feelings are the primary reason we do anything. They are the primary drivers of human behavior. When your emotions are on your side, it becomes natural to take action.

On the other hand, logical thinking is ineffective when your emotions are opposing you. For example, suppose you have to do your taxes, but you are relaxing and watching the TV. Your mind is at rest and you are in no mood to do anything. It will be a LOT HARDER to logically convince yourself that you should turn off the TV and open your tax file.

It can be done, but chances of logic overcoming emotions are very slim.

This is where visualization comes into the picture. It aligns your emotions with your goals, so there is no friction between the two. How easy do you think it will be when your thoughts and emotions are on the same side? Going with the tax example, your thoughts would be telling you to do your taxes, and you feel an emotional compulsion to do it as well.

Now, what are your chances to turn off the TV and do your taxes?

Visualization is so effective that it sometimes feels like magic. Whether you believe in the law of attraction (as in 'the secret') or not, sometimes it seems as if visualization has more power than we understand.

There has been a lot of research been done on visualization in recent times and its positive effects have been widely accepted by the researchers worldwide. In fact, visualization is widely used by top athletes, entrepreneurs, success coaches, celebrities, and other people who are at the top in their respective field.

• Jim Carrey used visualization to achieve stardom and become a multi-millionaire in 5 years.

• Arnold Schwarzenegger had pictures and a poster of Reg Park, his idol. He constantly imagined his body shaping up like Reg's. In his own words "the more I focused in on this image and worked, the more I saw it was real and possible for me to be like him." He went on to become the most awarded bodybuilder of his time.

• Tiger Woods, the ultra-successful golfer, was taught to visualize by his father in his childhood and he used it ever since. During his matches, he visualizes the ball going exactly where he wants it to go and then make a shot. He became one of the most successful and wealthiest golfers in history.

• Will Smith, the famous Hollywood actor, gives a lot of credit for his success to visualization. In his mind, he always imagined himself as being an A-list Hollywood celebrity. He said- "in my mind, I was always a Hollywood superstar. You all just don't know it yet."

There are countless examples of successful people who used visualization to boost their motivation and conviction for their objectives. I personally vouch for the effectiveness of visualization. This book was pending for more than 1 year and somehow I always found a reason for not to work on it.

Frustrated at my behavior, I started visualizing regularly that my book is finished within 6 months time. Soon I started experiencing increased motivation to sit down and write. What's more, I started neglecting the previous excuses that used to stop me from writing. As a result, I completed this book in a little over 6 months.

I can go on about how visualization is one of the most life-changing tools we know, but I recommend reading Dr. Maltz's excellent book: *Psycho-cybernetics* if you want research behind visualization.

How to visualize: an easy, step-by-step guide?

1. First, sit or lie down in a relaxed, quiet environment. Make sure there are no distractions like excessive noise or lights. You should feel relaxed in this environment. For most people, such a place would be their bedroom.

2. Close your eyes. Take a few deep, relaxed breaths. Consciously relax your body and mind.

3. Once you are feeling relaxed, close your eyes. Start imagining that you have reached your goal. You have achieved what you wanted and are filled with excitement & joy. Imagine it in as much detail as possible. It should be easy because it's something you really want. You will start feeling really good.

Note: Don't worry. You don't have to do it perfectly. Just add as many details as you can. After little practice, you will be able to visualize in much more detail.

4. Now keep viewing that vision (and feeling good) for few moments (1 to 5 minutes).

5. Open your eyes and relax.

Wasn't that easy? And it's quite enjoyable too. You feel really good from mentally experiencing your desired goals.

Visualization is easy, enjoyable and VERY POWERFUL. Do it regularly, preferably before sleeping at night or soon after waking up in the morning because both the times your mind is very open to external suggestions. Another great time for visualization is after you finish your meditation.

Make the practice of visualization a daily habit and reap the rewards forever.

"If you do this for few minutes in a day, you change your whole day. But if you do this few minutes every day, you get a different life." **- Anthony Robbins,** life coach and entrepreneur.

4. Deliberate Exposure

Another quite effective way to reach a high motivation level is what I call "deliberate exposure".

Whenever you have some free time, immerse yourself in pictures, audio & information of your objective on daily basis. Read books, listen to audio, view pictures, read information about your selected goal.

For example, if your goal is to buy a brand new Volkswagen Jetta, read its reviews, go to its website, read glowing ownership experiences, watch long ride videos on YouTube, read about its earlier models and technical advancements.

As we go through our day, there are lots of things which demand our attention like work, family responsibilities, hobbies, friends, etc. Going through our daily grind, we tend to forget about our goal.

The human mind has a tendency to put things in the background if it's not something which demands immediate attention. And because goals normally require some time to accomplish, it tends to get 'out of focus' for the majority of the day. This causes a loss in the intensity of motivation.

Let's suppose you did positive affirmations on your goals this morning and are feeling pumped up. You feel intensely motivated and are raring to go. But later during the day, you get caught up in some other work-related issue or maybe a friend needs your urgent help.

It's very common to forget about your goal when you get caught up in the daily grind. It causes a loss in motivation and worse, you start to get thoughts like - "oh I cannot focus on my goals for long. Maybe I am just not cut out for this kind of thing" or "I keep forgetting about my goals, maybe they are not so important for me?"

"Always remember, your focus determines your reality." - **George Lucas**, filmmaker and entrepreneur.

It takes a toll on your feelings of desire. Slowly but surely, your motivation starts going down.

The solution is to deliberately, knowingly expose yourself to your desire so you can see it, hear it, and read about it. It will make sure your goals are in your mind all the time. Whenever you have some free time, instead of watching random music videos, watch something related to your goal- any new information, review, people's opinions, how other successful people achieved it and so on...

It can be a video, book, songs, audio program, pictures or anything else related to your goal. This is called "deliberate exposure." Dwelling on your desire. Immersing yourself in it.

But to clear things up... it does not mean that you should watch videos all day and not take action. Deliberate exposure is meant to be done in spare time, in place of other unneeded activities we do when we get free.

For example, you want to grow your business and have scheduled marketing work during 11 am to 4 pm, do not waste your precious work time by reading an article about the luxurious lifestyle of big business owners.

When it's time to work, do your work with full concentration. When you get some free time to do other activities, you can choose to spend it reading/watching anything about your desire.

It's your answer against distractions and negative influences. That's another positive aspect of 'Deliberate exposure'. It protects you from indulging in some activity which may cause you to be distracted for the whole day. It guards your mind against other negative influences like gossiping, reading rumors, wasting time on social media, because you are spending your free time focusing on your goal.

As you can imagine, deliberate exposure can boost your concentration, productivity, and motivation to a much higher level. In my own experience, it made my mind completely focused on my goals. Regardless of the activity I'd be doing, my goals were on my mind. I found it very effective. It truly made my mental focus stick to my desires all the time. The level of motivation I felt was unbelievable.

In a nutshell:

1. When you are working, put your complete attention on doing the best work possible.

2. In your free time, you should be doing the following:

   • Watch videos, movies, TV programs related to your goals.

   • Listen to songs, audiobooks, and podcasts on your chosen objective.

   • Read books, articles, news, and blogs to collect new information on your goals.

• Talk about it with open-minded people who support you and your cause.

• Create a vision board - a place where you keep different pictures of your goals.

Many people set a goal for themselves but not focus on it frequently. Deliberate exposure will keep your goal at the forefront of your mind and ensure your intensity of desire never fades.

Chapter #7

OVERCOMING YOUR GREATEST BARRIER

"I learned that courage is not absence of fear, but the triumph over it. The brave man is not he who does not feel afraid, but he who conquers that fear." - **Nelson Mandela**, political leader, revolutionary and philanthropist.

On your way to success, one of the biggest roadblocks you would have to overcome is fear. It stops people from believing in themselves, dreaming big, and going for what they want.

Each one of us is afraid. We all have fears. But anyone who became successful had to overcome their fears. There is no other way. If you don't take control of your fear, then fear will control you.

You need to have the upper hand here. Fear will always BLOCK you from making progress in life. When you are taking a step ahead, it will ALWAYS be there to stop you. And it will become even stronger as you get closer to the finish line.

I was surprised to know that even great public speakers feel 'fear' before giving their speech. Just like everyone, they too are afraid of going on stage. But they don't let the fear stop them... and that is what makes them "great".

Olivia Fox Cabane, the author of *The Charisma Myth*, reveals that she still deals with fear every time she goes on stage, even after 15 years of public speaking experience.

Fear will ALWAYS be there. You only learn to deal with it.

As you gain experience, you will realize that most of the time, your fears never come true. And when they actually do happen, it's NEVER as bad as you thought it would be.

False evidence appearing real

Some people say F.E.A.R is 'false evidence appearing real'. That's a nice acronym. It represents fear for what it actually is - prediction of a possible bad outcome.

We are so afraid that there is a possibility of experiencing a bad outcome, we never even do it, even if there are more chances of succeeding than failing. (Note: by the way, there is no such thing as failure. We will cover this in more detail in upcoming chapters.)

It's good to pay attention to your fears and get to know what they actually represent. Some fears are good for you. Fear of heights keeps you safe by not allowing you to do anything dangerous on heights. Fear of snakes and other dangerous animals is good for your wellbeing. Fears of fire, electricity, poisonous things are there to keep you safe.

Such kinds of fears are completely natural and even necessary. They keep you away from physical harm. They are good for you.

What we need is to push past fears which serve no purpose in today's modern society. Let's take the fear of public speaking for example. Researchers have conducted a survey on what's the scariest experience for people.

It turned out that people are more afraid of public speaking than death. What a shocker! Especially considering there's no actual physical harm involved in standing on stage and expressing your ideas.

But we tend to run negative mental movies in our mind which paralyze us. Have you seen someone shaking when they stand on stage? Is it a life-threatening situation? A tiger is coming to attack them on stage?

No.

Examine your fears and figure out which ones are good & which ones serve no purpose. Baseless fears like public speaking, being rejected, and being disliked are stopping you from living your dream life.

You must learn to deal with them in order to fulfill your dreams. People who fail to go past their fears get stuck in the same position for years. Ask anyone who made it big: what was the most important thing they did to reach the next level?

Almost always the answer would be - "overcoming my fears"

99.99% of the time, the sensation of fear is much worse than the actual bad outcome. We can deal with a difficult situation when we experience it. It's the fear of these difficulties that does more harm than the actual experience itself.

We imagine the situation to be 100 times worse than it actually is and play this negative movie in our minds repeatedly. It intensifies feelings of fear. And finally, when we confront the actual situation, our mind reacts the way we trained it till now - It feels terrified!

My early experience with fear

Let me share an example. In my childhood, I was a shy little kid. To increase my social confidence, my class teacher told me to read out a three-page essay in front of the whole class. I had three days to prepare.

Those three days felt like three centuries. I was so afraid of standing in front of people and their eyes looking at me, that I couldn't write one page of the essay.

I imagined all sorts of things- The whole class laughing at me, gossiping forever about how badly I did, no one talking to me, no friends, being alone forever... AND being laughed at for being alone.

It was the worst feeling ever!

On the third day, I silently went to the teacher's room and told her I am scared and couldn't write the essay because of it. My teacher understood it was my fear that needed to be dealt with.

She asked me to read only half-page that I wrote and go back to my seat. I was still terrified but had to do it.

After I did it, I swear it was not half as bad as I imagined. Nobody laughed, nobody shouted at me, nobody gossiped about me afterward, and my friends were still willing to talk to me.

The whole incident gave me confidence, but more importantly, taught me a lesson that the fear is worse than the actual situation itself. We tend to make fears bigger than they really are.

This is something I want you to realize as well. We over-amplify fears in our mind. The closer you move towards your fear, the smaller it would become.

The human brain is highly sensitive to the possibility of pain. Even if the chances of success and failure are equal - 50:50, we focus more on negative 50%. In worse cases (people with negative attitude, depression etc) mind tend to focus on negative even if the chances of a positive outcome are much higher, say 80:20.

To be massively successful, we deliberately have to train our mind to focus on the positive side of things. Because, by default, the mind will focus on pain more than pleasure, negative more than positive.

There are a lot of factors involved in forming this 'negative-focus': bad childhood experiences, family atmosphere, upbringing, the attitude of surrounding people, friends, peers, influences like TV, news etc - all play a part in training your mind to focus primarily on the negative.

And that's not all. There is a biological reason behind the tendency of mind to focus more on the negative. In the caveman times, when the human brain was still developing, the survival was very difficult. The choices we made were the difference between life and death.

It was more important to anticipate and avoid danger than gaining feelings of pleasure. Avoiding confrontation with a sabertooth tiger was preferred over than finding food that may be found in the area.

In those harsh conditions, the human mind developed a tendency to focus more on negative than positive. Since then, the world has changed around us. Conditions are much more favorable now, but we still have that same "safety" mechanism inside us. We continue to focus more on negatives to avoid any 'possible' bad outcomes.

So, you MUST become comfortable with being afraid. Fear will ALWAYS be there, at every corner of life. There is no running away from it. You are hardwired to experience fear.

But the interesting thing is, the majority of your fears (public speaking, social anxiety, being embarrassed, rejection, etc) are invalid today. They serve no purpose. If you want to be successful in this day & age, you have to push past your fears.

When you overcome your fears, success is a few inches away.

In order to live the life of your dreams, you need to learn HOW to move past your fears. And that's the main focus of this chapter. We are going to discuss some extremely effective ways to banish any fear that's holding you back.

How to overcome fear?

The techniques below are some of the most effective ways to reduce or even completely eliminate fear. These are the ones which I found to make the biggest positive impact against being afraid. I would like to share them with you now.

I came up with this list after ready hundreds of books, listening to audio programs, watching videos, attending seminars on fear and testing their effectiveness on myself and other people.

Some of these techniques are backed up by real-world research, while some are 'words of wisdom' that proved to be extremely helpful in real life.

Instead of choosing between modern science and old wisdom... I included them both here because I believe there's something we can learn from each side.

So let's start with the first:

1. Face your fears

A friend of mine used to be terrified at the thought of speaking in front of the audience. We were doing MBA together and all of us had to give a presentation on a pre-selected topic. He was very nervous night before giving his first presentation.

I tried to explain to him that there is nothing to be afraid of. But it was of no use. Emotions tend to override logic every time. The next day, he was very nervous, literally shaking on stage. He fumbled his words, had poor eye contact, and was not engaging at all.

People in the audience felt bad for him because he normally was a friendly guy with a sharp mind.

After this not-so-great first experience, my friend was determined to get this handled, but he was still afraid of speaking on stage. Fortunately for him, as MBA students, we were called to give presentations again.

This time, my friend looked less afraid on stage than before, and when we pointed it out to him afterward, he felt better.

In the next several presentations he gave, his fear gradually kept diminishing. All of a sudden, he was starting to speak louder, displaying confident body language and being more expressive & engaging as a speaker.

Till the end of two year period, he became one of the best in college at presentations.

This experience taught me that exposing yourself repeatedly to your fears actually lower their intensity. Is my friend still a little nervous before going on stage?

Yes.

But he has done it so many times, it now feels more like excitement than fear. He says, "Exposing yourself to your fear takes the sting out of it and makes it quite manageable."

This is a thoroughly researched phenomenon. Read *Face the fear and do it anyway* by Susan Jeffers. It's an excellent book on this particular topic.

2. Having a strong faith

One of the core pillars of strength against fear is faith. Have a strong faith in yourself, your vision and ability to succeed. A strong, unshakable faith can move mountains and a weak one can stop you from taking even the first step.

Realize that every man on earth is created equal. The richest and the most successful people have the same brain and physical structure as you have. Nobody is cut from a different cloth.

We all have the same brain, body, abilities, energy and time. The basic foundation is the same for everyone. It's the way you use what you have been given makes all the difference.

"If you never try, you'll never know what you are capable of." - **John Barrow**, English physicist.

Successful people use their resources on things like reading, training, taking action, finding solutions, making progress etc.

Using their resources in a positive direction is what separates the best from the rest.

So believe in yourself and your vision. Right now, at this very moment, you have all the resources to become the most successful, richest, amazing person in the world. You are more than enough, this very moment. You are not realizing your own potential.

Think BIG!

Go for greater goals!

Have UNSHAKABLE faith!

It's all about how strong your faith is. The conviction with which you believe in yourself. Your faith, at any point, should never be anything less than unbreakable.

There are two reasons for it. 1) Nobody is cut from a different cloth. You have exact same resources as the ultra-successful people. 2) a breakable faith is of no use at all.

The bigger your goal, the stronger your faith needs to be. Bigger goals need more time and effort. They also contain harder challenges. In such cases, it's critical to operate with unshakable faith because it will be tested many times over!

"*None of us know what might happen even the next minute, yet still we go forward. Because we trust. Because we have faith.*" - **Paulo Coelho**, author of *The Alchemist*.

When all else fails, you can come back to your faith to take shelter from chaos & uncertainty. It's like an oasis in the vast desert. It is your place of certainty and calm. A strong faith has the power to keep you going even when it seems like all doors are closed.

Faith keeps you going...

Faith and fear cannot co-exist together. They cancel each other out. In your mind, there is place for only one - faith or fear. And you get to decide which one exists. You are the creator of both faith and fear. You have complete power over their existence.

Many people don't realize they are creators of both. Use this gift in your favor.

"*Faith and fear both have you believing in something which you cannot see... You decide.*" -**Bob Proctor,** world renowned speaker and author.

Always have complete faith in yourself, your abilities and a positive future. There is no reason you shouldn't. A lack of faith will weaken your resolve and ensure that you quit at the very first signs of difficulty and setback.

On the other hand, an unshakable faith will guide you towards the life of your dreams. Now that we established the importance of having a strong faith, let's look at how to develop and maintain faith.

How to strengthen your faith?

1- Start with your "why"

Identify the reasons for which you want what you want. If your "why" is important enough, you will keep a much stronger level of faith. You have to really believe in the reason for which you want to succeed.

When your reasons are critically important, you simply cannot afford to lose. The level of your desire is a big influence on how strong your faith is. So really connect yourself with your "why". Become attached to it emotionally. Feel its importance.

It will make you desire your goals so much that you won't even consider any possibility of it not happening.

2- Positive affirmations

They have been proven time and again to be very beneficial for maintaining high levels of faith. Your mind is like a sponge. It starts to believe any thought which gets repeated on a frequent basis. Use this power to your advantage. Affirmations are super effective. For details on how to do affirmations correctly, check out chapter 3: Beliefs.

3- Past success

If you have achieved success in the past, you tend to have greater faith in yourself. If you have been successful, take time to remember how you felt, how you thought and what you did.

Remembering your success in a positive light will create faith in your mind - "I have dealt with many obstacles before and have been successful. I will make it this time as well."

4- Everyone is equal

Knowing that successful people are just like you, have the same abilities, challenges and energy will strengthen your resolve. Many ultra-successful people have started their journey from a very low position - being broke, unhealthy, no education, no support, etc. If you are reasonably educated, healthy and have enough time to read this book, you have a much better starting point.

5- Small progress

Your faith gets stronger as you take action and start making progress. People say they don't have enough faith to take action. They don't realize that as you take action and start seeing some progress, your faith starts becoming stronger.

With your increased faith, you take even more action which gets you even better results, which further strengthens your faith. It's like a continuous, upward cycle of strengthening faith.

6- Faith in God/Universe

Another strong source of faith is the feeling that some greater force is watching over you and if you give your best, it will be repaid. Religious people think of such greater force as God. If you are an atheist, you can think of it as greater good or the universe.

Faith in some other greater entity will make you relaxed and calm. When you believe there is a sense of justice in the world and your efforts are being taken into account, you won't be too worried about the result. You will do your best and have faith.

"Your duty is to make your best effort, without worrying about the result... result will come." **-Lord Krishna**

7. Mental practice

The third extremely effective way to banish fear is by mental practice. Suppose you are afraid of going up to your boss and ask for a raise. Whenever you think about the scenario you imagine his frowning eyes, tensed lips and, "about-to-burst" vibe.

This creates fear in your mind. The actual scenario hasn't happened yet, but you imagined it would go badly.

There has been a lot of research done in this area in the last few decades. It has been found that the mind cannot tell the difference between real life and something imagined in detail.

As you imagine bad outcomes (i.e. your boss getting angry at you for asking for a raise) your mind responds as if it happened in the past. Consequently, fear is created to prevent you from doing that again.

The fear cycle goes like this:

Negative outcome imagined--> mind believes it --> fear is created.

We need to break this cycle and turn it around so it helps us achieve what we want. Let's take the same 'asking for a raise' example.

The night before you meet your boss, imagine you are walking into your boss's cabin with a smile on your face. Your boss greets you warmly. You start out with a friendly chat, then in a very relaxed, confident manner tell him that you think you deserve a raise.

Your boss looks receptive to the idea. You show him your last year's performance data and information on the current market value of someone with your experience. Your boss looks at the data you provided and agrees.

You exchange some pleasantries, shake hands and walk out triumphant.

If you repeat this imagination several times, your mind will accept it as truth. Your fears will completely banish or get reduced to a minimum. You will have a much stronger belief in a positive outcome.

Best of all, when you do go up to your boss, you'll feel like you have done this several times before and the positive outcome has already happened. You will feel a lot more confident and self-assured. Other people (in this case, your boss) will really feel your positive energy and confidence and you will have a much higher chance of getting success.

This is called MENTAL PRACTICE.

It is a thoroughly researched and proven way to eliminate fear and improve the performance of an individual. We know that the subconscious mind cannot differentiate between real and imagined. We can use it to our advantage.

If we imagine doing an activity in vivid detail, mind accepts it as a real-life event and records it in our memory. The more mental practice you do, the better you adjust to it in real life. This has a tremendous impact on fear.

If you repeatedly imagine - doing something you fear and obtaining a positive outcome from it, your fear will disappear.

It was believed that the human body cannot run fast enough to cover a mile in four minutes. Nobody in history was able to do it. As a shocker for the medical world, Robert Banister was able to run a mile within four minutes.

When he was asked how he prepared for it, Robert said he regularly imagined running a mile under four minutes. He couldn't do it in the real world, so he did it enough times in his mind.

This removed the limitations and fear of failure from his mind. He completely believed that he would be able to do it and his body got him through.

That is one of the most inspirational stories I know that proves mental practice can eliminate fear and improve your performance.

And the best of all, it is very easy to do and requires nothing but a few minutes of your time.

How to perform mental practice?

1. Take something you really are afraid of (I.e. Public speaking, being rejected, failure in business etc.)

2. Find a quiet, comfortable place.

3. Lie down and close your eyes.

4. Take 5-10 deep breaths. Relax your body.

5. Now start imagining yourself doing the activity. See yourself doing a good job. People are smiling at you. You are feeling confident.

6. Next, see yourself succeeding in your goal. You have achieved your outcome (I.e. You got the raise, your business is bringing lot's of profit, gave an extraordinary speech, etc)

7. Really try to imagine it as vividly as possible. It means adding sounds, lights, color, touch and feelings to your imagination. Try to include all five of these senses in your mental practice.

8. Immerse yourself in your imagination emotionally. Really FEEL good about it.

9. Continue for 10 minutes.

That's it.

People are amazed at how something so simple, can be so powerful. If you are dealing with fear in any area of life, use mental practice and other tools mentioned in this chapter to effectively deal with it.

I have personally tested several methods to deal with fear and these are the best I have found. Use what you have learned here to blast away your fears because they are nothing but self-imposed limitations.

Many people, exactly like you, don't have "your" fears.

So why should you have them?

Chapter #8

THE MISSING KEY TO SUCCESS

Persistence defined

Persistence is the ability to keep moving forward, refusing to quit. It's among the most important qualities to have for achieving great success. It's is one of the missing keys to success for many people.

If you ask people who are at the top of their chosen field, they will tell you that persistence is among the top five most important qualities for becoming successful.

But many people are not persistent. They are not willing to deal with setbacks. They cannot imagine themselves moving forward when confronted with obstacles.

It's a shame because if someone is willing to deal with obstacles in his/her path, success is usually not far away. They just need to keep going.

On the other hand, some people ARE persistent. They believe in moving forward. They are willing to tackle any problems in their path. Such people enviably become ultra-successful in life and people around them look at them as a source of inspiration.

Stephen King persistence

While writing his first published book, Carrie, Stephen King threw the first few pages of the book in the trash. His wife took them out of the trash and requested him to continue. He continued writing, and the rest is history.

Now, even adults fear clowns...

Persistence help shape a person's character. Developing the skill of persistence can turn weak men into emotionally balanced, strong individuals. It actually takes a lot of internal strength and maturity to be persistent. People like that have an aura of calm confidence. They believe they can deal with any challenge, and do not get unsettled when facing adversity.

People around can sense their confidence and respect them for it.

This internal strength can only come from within. It is something which cannot be faked. It comes from constantly walking your path in life and dealing with obstacles as they arise; it takes effort, along with discipline, to be persistent.

And you must be willing to pay that price. It's not easy, but the payoff —whether financial or otherwise —is manifold greater than the efforts you put in. Look at any successful person around you: they had to show a huge amount of persistence to be where they are right now.

This world has always rewarded people who showed persistence and will continue to do so in the future.

Thomas Edison persistence

The greatest inventor in history had to fail 10,000 times before he was able to create the light bulb. If he hadn't shown persistence, we would still be sitting by candlelight. About this persistence, he said, "If I find 10,000 ways something doesn't work, I haven't failed. I am not discouraged because every wrong attempt discarded is another step forward."

There are no shortcuts. Nothing can replace persistence; it is non-negotiable for achieving great success. It's never a question of "if" persistence is important, it's "how much" persistence you need to have.

The amount of persistence you must have depends largely on the size of your goal. The bigger, more ambitious your goal, the more persistent you need to be. Bigger goals normally contain more challenges, so your resolve gets tested more often.

How persistence shapes character?

Think of this persistence as a rite of passage. Traditionally, young men had to go through a specific and difficult test to prove themselves. Upon successful completion, they were accepted in their tribe as warriors and commanded equal respect as other honored members.

In our society, you don't have to kill a tiger with a spear to prove yourself, but you should have your own personal mission and its unique rite of passage. You are the one walking your path and this is a test you must go through before achieving greatness.

People say being persistent is uncomfortable, but I look at it as purification of spirit. When you face constant challenges and push through them, the pain and discomfort kill any weakness in your mind and character.

Just as physical exercise makes muscles stronger, pain strengthens your character. Those who go through hardships and still move forward are revered as modern-day warriors.

Another positive side of being persistent is that you enjoy the result more if you had to work for it. Everyone likes freebies, but their enjoyment does not last long. People forget about it as soon as their attention finds the next shiny thing.

The opposite is true when you have to use a lot of effort to obtain your goal. It then becomes more than just a result, it becomes an achievement, a life-long reminder of your feat. When you think about it, you remember all the hardships you had to suffer through, and your determination to keep on going until you found your strength. That really is an achievement!

I too have been through a lot, and let me tell you, when I look back, the memories I'm most proud of are the ones where I had to challenge myself to achieve something I intensely desired.

For me personally, it's the best feeling in the world.

"Fall down seven times, get up eight" —**Japanese proverb**

You must accept the fact that setbacks, hardships, and failures will always be there. You will face them at every corner of your journey to success. There's no easy route, no shortcut. Success is a result of consistent effort sustained over a period of time. Those who go looking for a magic pill come back disappointed.

Don't be afraid to fail. It's nothing but an indication that you need to change your approach. Failure and rejections are an inseparable part of success. They highlight what you're doing wrong and force you to correct your actions.

"Being challenged in life is inevitable; being defeated is optional" —**Roger Crawford,** renowned motivational speaker and author.

You must be willing to go through setbacks if you wish to succeed. And persistence enables you to convert failures into achievements.

As long as you learn from your mistakes and move forward, nothing can stop you from reaching your destination. It's like continuously pouring single drops of water into a glass. It may not seem to make a difference at first, but over time, the glass SURELY gets filled. No matter how wild and outlandish your goal is, as long as you don't stop, it may take time, but you WILL get there.

All the tools and principles mentioned in this book are valuable only if you are persistent in their application. If you only try once or twice and then stop, nothing I say or show will be of any use.

It's like learning to walk. You do it, and then you fall. You get up again, walk a bit, and then fall. You get better the more you do it, IN SPITE OF FALLING. That's the kind of attitude you must have toward success and learning.

Make persistence a habit. And what's the best way to make persistence a habit? Start small, and then build up. For example, try waking up early each day, then make exercise a regular activity, and then start doing 15–20 minutes of meditation every day.

Small things like this will build up your "persistence muscles". Like any other behavior, persistence gets stronger with use and gets weaker with disuse. Even small things like regularly taking time for a five-minute walk in the morning can help strengthen your persistence habit.

The more you do it, the easier it gets to "be persistent".

It's worth developing persistence because its benefits will pay off in all areas of your life: business, finance, relationships, health, self-development, spirituality, love, etc. This single quality will change your life in more ways than you would believe.

Research shows there's a big difference between the average American and the top 1% of the population. The average annual income of the top 1% is $717,000, while the average annual income of the rest of the country is $51,000.

There's even a sub-set in that 1%. At the bottom are professionals like doctors and lawyers who earn an average annual income of $300,000, while the most successful people earn over $27 million.

Many of them are self-made millionaires who had to start from nothing and build their way up to the upper echelons of society. You can imagine the kinds of challenges they had to face and the amount of persistence they had to show to reach that position.

They are no different from you and me. We are all the same. The difference is they had a vision and were persistent enough in their efforts.

On that note, we've thoroughly covered why persistence is a must. Now, we're going to look at some of the most powerful tools to build persistence so it becomes a part of "who we are".

How to be more persistent?

1. Discipline

Persistence requires energy. While working, be very disciplined. Be extremely careful with your time and energy. Define your priorities and focus only on them. Be aware of things that do not help you in any way. Stop wasting time on TV, playing video games, reading magazines, drinking alcohol, and eating nutritionally empty foods. Cut out any other activity that is taking up your time and energy and do nothing beneficial for you.

As you take breaks in between periods of action, be very careful about how you recover your energy. People often start watching TV when they take a break. Ask yourself if you have more energy or less after watching an hour of television.

A break is meant to recharge you, not distract you. Things like TV are energy drainers that can delay further action. Be disciplined and completely stop indulging in ANY activity that wastes your energy and time.

This will let you maintain a precious reserve of energy that you will be using for valuable things like taking action, concentrating, brainstorming, and persisting.

Discipline also helps you fight negative, self-defeating thoughts. Disciplined people are not only externally disciplined; they are internally disciplined as well. When you have negative thoughts, be disciplined enough to ignore them and trust that things will work out the way you want. You will be a lot more persistent.

2. Persistence and motivation

Motivation fuels persistence. The more intensely you desire something, the more you will be willing to push through obstacles. Motivation is such an important component of being persistent that it can be thought of as the source from which your willingness to move forward originate.

Without motivation, no one will persist. Why anyone would want to deal with problems for no reason at all?

Your reasons (for which you want your goals) are the source of your grit. They provide infinite energy and willingness to push past roadblocks. The more you want something, the further you would be willing to go for it.

Your level of persistence will always be proportional to your level of motivation. Increase your motivation, and your level of persistence will increase as well.

In this book, I have devoted an entire chapter on creating and maintaining high levels of motivation. Chapter 6 contains various tools and methods to help you do just that. As you get accustomed to high levels of motivation, you will find that you are much more willing to push through problems in your path.

3. Momentum

Momentum stands for the flow you have when you are taking action on a consistent basis. It's like if you are already going to the gym 5 days a week, it will be much easier to work out 6 days a week. Because you are already taking action, you have a certain momentum. It's much easier to keep a ball rolling, then to get it moving from a standstill.

That's why starting something new is harder than keeping it going. It takes a lot more effort to initiate something. But once it picks up momentum, it'll be much easier to maintain.

This is very helpful in being persistent. If you are just starting out and want to develop persistence, do small tasks which demand little persistence from you. For example, start drinking green tea every day and be persistent with that, start going out jogging every day, stop wasting time on TV & useless websites.

Take it easy in the beginning. Start small and do activities which require only little persistence. Once you get comfortable, begin taking up challenges which require more. For example, eating healthy, exercising regularly, sticking to your schedule, taking action, etc.

As you successfully complete smaller challenges, you will start gaining momentum. It will become increasingly easier to persist. And as you keep challenging yourself with more and more tasks, your momentum will get stronger. Soon, you will reach a point where it will be easier to be persistent than to stop.

And this will have a spill-over effect on all areas of your life. Momentum is energy, and by practicing it, you are putting energy in your everyday life. You will feel more alive and vibrant. The joy of taking down challenges, coupled with satisfaction from moving in the direction of your desires will create such a high, you will not want to stop.

At such a point, the power of momentum is really on your side. You will breeze past any obstacles & problems without giving a second thought. It's like shifting to the fast lane to success. Moving forward will become your default way of thinking and behaving.

But you have to be careful as well. Just as the momentum is gained by taking action, it can decrease or even die out if you stop. You have to keep taking action regularly to build and sustain healthy levels of momentum. Do not think once you gain momentum, it will continue on its own forever. If you stop, momentum will start decreasing, and with time, it will fade away.

So have both of these factors in mind - a) taking frequent action creates and sustains momentum. b) being stagnant will kill momentum.

Use this knowledge to your advantage and never lose your momentum. The higher your momentum, the stronger your persistence would be.

Success story of Sylvester Stallone

Sylvester Stallone, we all know him as one of Hollywood's greatest actors, but many people don't know the sacrifices he made to reach stardom. His incredible journey to success and stardom stands as an inspiration for the whole world.

Ever since his childhood, Sylvester Stallone wanted to be a movie star. It was his big dream. He had troubled family life when he was a kid and moved out as soon as he could. He never wanted to do a normal 9-to-5 job, as it would kill his desire for an acting career.

He tried a bunch of minor acting roles but never got anything big out of them. And at the time, he was completely broke. His wife used to argue with him to get a normal job like other people. He didn't, because he believed it would lower his hunger for showbiz.

Their financial situation got so bad that he stole his wife's jewelry and sold it. That was the end of their relationship. After that, he had no money to pay for rent, so he had to live on the streets for days.

The lowest point came when he had to sell his beloved dog, whom he loved most of all, to a guy in front of a liquor store. He said he walked away and cried.

Two weeks later he was watching a boxing match between Mohammed Ali and Chuck Wepner. The fight gave him inspiration to write the script for movie - ROCKEY. After the fight, he started writing. He wrote for 20 hours straight and completed the entire script for Rocky in one go.

Then he went to hundreds of movie agents in New York, only to be rejected again and again. But he never gave up. His desire and the will to persist kept him going. Finally, a studio agreed to make the movie.

But there was still one problem...

He wanted to be the star of the movie himself. He wanted to play the lead role of Rocky. But the studio did not agree. They wanted a 'real' star. They didn't think Stallone was fit for the lead role.

They offered him $125,000 for the script but did not want to him in the lead role. Stallone refused.

Here is a man with no money... completely broke, and still turned away $125,000 because he had a vision - to be the star himself - and a willingness to persist.

A few weeks later, they came back and offered him $250,000 for the script. He said "not without me starring in the lead role". They refused.

They again came back and offered him $350,000 for the script.

He turned down $350,000...

Finally, the studio compromised and Stallone was allowed to play in the lead role, but with a cut in payment - only $35,000.

The movie turned out to be a Mega-Hit, grossing $225 million in the global box office receipts and went on to become the highest grossing film of 1976. It won the hearts of people all over and was nominated for nine categories in Academy Awards. Won three for best picture, best director and best film editing.

This unbelievable story of a man's heart and persistence stands as a testimonial for the fact that even incredibly hard situations & obstacles can be overcome if one has the desire to succeed, and a willingness to persist with all his strength.

Chapter #9

HOW TO ENSURE YOUR SUCCESS

"I can accept failure, everyone fails at something. But I can't accept not trying." - **Michael Jordan**, basketball legend.

People are afraid to fail. Many give up even before they take the first step. Thoughts like "What's the use?", "Why try? I will never get that", "It's beyond my abilities" and "I have never achieved something like this before"; race through their minds every time they go after a BIG goal.

It's very common to experience thoughts like that. All people experience fear and doubts, especially when they go after a goal which is beyond their past achievements.

But what if I tell you that you can ENSURE your success one hundred percent, and there is no such thing as a failure?

Let me introduce you to the concept of embracing change.

Embrace change defined

Contrary to what people may believe, failure is not the end of the road to success. Failure is an indicator that you need to try something different to obtain your goal. You need to change your approach; do something different if your current plan is not working, and keep trying out different approaches/plans/actions until you find something which works.

Let's suppose you are trying to get in shape. You're going to the gym six times a week and following a healthy diet plan, but still not able to lose weight. Instead of getting disheartened, collect more information - consult your dietitian, read the best books on weight loss, etc.

Find out how the human body works, how we put on fat and how fat is converted into energy. Find out different forms of exercises like high-intensity interval training, cross-fit, etc. New information would show you several different ways to lose weight.

Pick any one. Make changes in your diet and exercise routine and continue it for a month or two. Look for the progress. If you don't see any improvement, make changes in your diet and exercise program yet again.

Stick to it, and look for the results. Rinse and repeat until you find a diet & exercise plan which works for you.

Success is virtually GUARANTEED if you keep trying different approaches to obtain your objective. The ONLY way you cannot succeed, is when you CHOOSE to stop trying.

"*You must change your approach in order to change your results.*" - **Jim Rohn**, entrepreneur, author and motivational speaker.

Success is like finding combination of a lock. You may need to try a few different combinations, but if you persist, you'll eventually get the lock open. Persistence, when combined with changing your approach, is the recipe for guaranteed success.

Some people may ask, "But how do I find other approach options? How would I know what to try next?"

We live in an age where information is available at every moment. There are thousands of books, eBooks, YouTube videos, seminars, audio programs, blogs, newsletters, CD and DVD programs, podcasts and other sources available to you right now. Take advantage of them. Learn.

Most successful people in the world are constant learners. They never stop learning. Bill Gates was a college dropout who became one of the richest people in the world. He attributes the majority of his success to being a constant learner.

Research repeatedly shows that learning and constantly improving yourself are much more powerful predictors of success than a college degree. While it's great to have a college degree, you need to become a student for life.

When you learn, you grow. When you think you've made it and stop learning, you start going downhill.

Anthony Robbins said, "In this world, nothing is constant. Either you are growing or dying." Always keep educating yourself. You can find people who have accomplished a lot but are still learning new things every day.

Whatever your challenges may be, if you look for a solution, you will find it. Look around, it blows my mind that we can get millions of dollars' worth of information in a $10 soft-cover book!

Incredibly successful people, who have spent their lifetime overcoming challenges, wrote all their knowledge and experience in a little book... and you have access to it! You are fortunate enough to learn what they learned in about a fraction of the time it took them to discover all these solutions.

We are blessed to live in times like this. Think about it. You have a massive advantage over previous generations which didn't have the kinds of resources available to you now.

Learn and use this knowledge. You would discover several options to reach your destination. Pick any one, and start taking action. Look for progress and make changes if required.

Each individual who became successful had to embrace change. Whether they had to change their attitude, behavior, plans, action, team or something similar, it's the "change" that ultimately brought them success.

I personally attribute 90% of my success to persistence and embracing change. Success never came easy for me. I always had to work harder than most people to achieve results.

At first, I used to get frustrated about it. "Why do I always have to work this much?" I would often ask myself, "Other people seem to get by with much less effort."

But my struggles turned out to be a blessing in disguise. It forced me to analyze what I was doing wrong and learn the fundamentals of success. I spent many years studying success and created a blueprint that can be applied to become successful in ANY endeavor. You have that blueprint in your hands right now.

Later, I realized that I can use this knowledge to help other people overcome their challenges as well. It led to the creation of my blog and books.

According to the evolution theory presented by Charles Darwin, species that are unable to adapt to constant change are likely to be weeded out of existence. This adaptation – change – is even more important now because our society is changing and evolving at a rapid pace.

In this day & age, businesses as well as individuals, have to change constantly in order to keep up with the pace of modern evolution. Those who fail, become "extinct". Successful businesses go down, people lose their wealth, top athletes get kicked out of the competition - all because they failed to change.

On the other hand, people and businesses who DO adapt themselves to the current situation become leaders of their chosen fields. Think about the most successful individuals and corporations. Can you count how many times they had to change in order to make progress?

The popular wisdom of 'don't quit' may not enough anymore. Even if you keep going, you're still in danger of doing the same ol' thing over and over again. It's like beating a dead horse.

You must combine 'don't quit' ideology with 'embracing change' in order to become wildly successful in your life.

Do not quit + embrace change = success is guaranteed

In the past, I too fell in the trap of doing things repeatedly which didn't work, while expecting a different result. As if a magic fairy would appear and say, "you poor soul; you've worked hard enough. I will give you what you want."

In life, success will never come from doing the WRONG things, no matter how persistent or hard-working you are.

But when you combine persistence with the willingness to change... boom!

You will succeed.

Every time.

Failure as feedback

Whenever you achieve any result, it's a feedback – either negative or positive. Positive feedback indicates, "You are going in the right direction. Keep going."

Negative feedback – failure or setback – represents, "Stop. Something is not right. It needs correction."

Always remember: when you experience failure, there is nothing to be ashamed of. You did your best at the time. Let it go and move forward. It may not feel good, but failure plays an important part in achieving success. Successful people are willing to fail more than other people in order to succeed.

"*I have missed more than 9,000 shots in my career. I have lost almost 300 games. 26 times, I have been trusted to take the game winning shot and missed. I have failed over and over again in my life. And that is why I succeed.*" **–Michael Jordan**, basketball legend.

Any feedback, whether it FEELS good or not, contains very valuable information. It indicates if you are on the right course or not. It also highlights the need to make necessary adjustments in your plans & activities required to move forward.

Think of negative feedback (a.k.a. failure) as a clue. Instead of quitting, look at what isn't working and change it. Embrace change to such an extent that you are CONSTANTLY SEEKING feedback.

Once you start collecting feedback quickly and make the necessary corrections, you'll progress at a rapid pace. All the underlying issues will surface quickly and be dealt with. This constant refinement will make your process much smoother and efficient. Soon, you will be cruising towards success.

"Failing forward is the ability to get back up after you have been knocked down, learn from your mistake, and move forward in a better direction." **–John C. Maxwell**, success coach.

Now, instead of being afraid of failure, think of it as feedback and a necessary component of success. Every successful person had to go through challenges and failure, but they looked at it as an opportunity. You must too.

Remove the whole concept of failure from your mind. There is no such thing as failure. There is only feedback.

The ONLY way you cannot succeed... is when you stop trying.

Keep moving and you will reach your destination... every time.

It's a very liberating feeling. How would you feel when you know you cannot fail, EVER? What would you achieve? What kind of goals would you go for?

Success story of Soichiro Honda

In 1930, when Japan was taken away by the Great Depression, Soichiro Honda was still in school. In 1937, he started developing 'piston rings' in a small workshop.

He wanted to sell the idea to Toyota and worked extremely hard for it. After working day and night, Honda was finally able to complete his piston rings and took a working sample to Toyota for examination.

Toyota rejected his piston rings. Reason: it did not meet their quality standards!

He went back to school where other engineers made fun of him, but he didn't give up. For two more years, Honda worked relentlessly on the design and refinement of his piston rings.

He submitted them again to Toyota and this time won a contract!

Now, he needed a factory to supply materials to Toyota. Unfortunately, Japan was gearing for war at the time, and resources were in short supply. He couldn't find enough cement to build his factory, so he developed a new process to create cement himself!

Soon the factory was constructed and was ready to begin production. But fate had other ideas. His factory was bombed twice, and steel became unavailable at the same time.

It really tested the resolve of Soichiro Honda. But he still didn't quit, only changed his approach.

He collected gasoline cans discarded by US fighters and started using them as new raw materials in his newly rebuilt manufacturing process.

As things started to look better, an earthquake leveled his factory yet again. Any ordinary person would have given up at that point. But he persisted.

After the war, there was a huge shortage of gasoline in Japan. People began to either walk or ride their bicycle to their destination. Honda saw an opportunity and attached a tiny engine to his bicycle.

His neighbors saw it and requested one for themselves. Honda tried to meet the demands, but he couldn't, as resources like material and money were lacking.

Instead of being disappointed, he looked for possible solutions.

He wrote an inspiring letter to 18,000 bicycle shop owners to help him revitalize Japan by innovation. Out of which 5,000 responded and forwarded whatever resources they could to him.

Then he began developing small bicycle engines. Initial ones were bulky and didn't work. After continuous refinement and development, however, he created a small engine "the super club" which became quite successful.

Soon, he began exporting his bicycle engines to Europe and America, establishing the brand of Honda overseas.

Later, when the world was moving towards small cars, Honda saw an opportunity and started manufacturing small cars. His expertise in creating small engines paid dividends and Honda cars became a runaway success.

Today, the Honda Corporation has more than 175,000 employees on multiple continents and became one of the largest automobile companies in the world.

All because of Soichiro Honda's willingness to learn, take action, change approach and a firm commitment to his dream...

Chapter #10

FINAL PIECES OF THE PUZZLE

As I mentioned earlier, this book is meant to be used as a reference guide. Any time you need a refresher, or solution of a specific problem, come back and re-read the related section.

In your journey to success, you would enviably come across various problems. Any time you feel stuck, remember to not get discouraged. You only need new knowledge or skill.

For example, you successfully get your new business up and running, but are having problems with handling cash flow, then you need to learn about how to manage your finances. You need to sit down and read finance books, attend local finance workshops, take guidance from experts, etc.

There's ALWAYS a way to get around your problem.

Have a mindset of being a student forever, and never stop learning. Think of it as a long term commitment to success. In order to become successful, it's required from you.

Don't think of it as a chore. In reality, it feels extremely GOOD to find solutions and overcome the challenges you are facing. It's a very liberating feeling.

Once you figured out how to solve a problem, you NEVER have to worry about it again. It's like finding a combination of a lock. Once you find it, you are good for life.

As you do this, you will experience MASSIVE amounts of success, and as a spillover effect, you become a LOT more confident in your everyday life.

Can you imagine how confident you would be when you know there is ALWAYS a way and you can find it?

Success is similar to the stock market. The more you put in, the more you shall receive. And if you worked intelligently, you shall receive much more than what you put in.

Careful planning and execution are crucial if you want to reach the next level. Some people think they reached the top. There is nothing more.

I believe there is always a next level. No matter how big you get, there is always a chance to grow.

Stop looking at your competitors and the people around you.

Compete only with yourself. No one else. The ONLY challenge you should be looking to beat is your own limit.

Always keep growing and improving yourself. Never stop.

This world needs you to be your best self.

By being your best, you will inspire other people to do the same. Become a pillar of positivity and strength for your society.

Be the sunlight that burns away the darkness from people's life.

Think of how much good you can do for others when you have the means, time and energy to do so.

Obtaining success is not selfish. It's your right. It's the best thing you can do to make this world a better place.

I wish you the best!

- Vishal Pandey

"If you found this book helpful, please take a moment of your time to put a review on the website from where you have purchased this book. Your review will be very valuable for getting this book to reach more people who need this information."

ABOUT THE AUTHOR

Vishal Pandey, author & publisher, was born in Lucknow, India. After completing post graduation in management, he joined the corporate world, only to realize quickly that it was not the path for him. His decade-old passion for self-development led him to the world of writing and creation of his blog.

Over the course of fourteen years, he read hundreds of books, listened to audio/video programs, attended seminars on the topic of personal development and tested every piece of information by applying it in real life.

His blog was originally created to share this information with the world but later evolved into a platform for mutual interaction with his readers. After receiving several requests to write a book from his readers, he wrote 'Positive Thinking', followed by 'Happiness Edge' and more.

Besides writing, he loves meditation, yoga, martial arts, music, nutrition, psychology, and travelling.

You can contact him at:

Email: yourselfactualization@gmail.com

Facebook: facebook.com/selfactualization.co

Twitter: @selfactualized9

MORE BOOKS BY VISHAL PANDEY

Positive Thinking: What It Really Takes To Free Yourself from Negativity

The Happiness Edge: The Eight Principles of Happiness to Gain Competitive Advantage in Business and Life

Happiness for Beginners

Social Success: Be Likeable, Create Instant Rapport and Influence People

The Magic of Positive Thinking

Gratitude: Getting In Touch With What Really Matters

Forgiveness: The Greatest Cure for a Suffering Heart

Happiness Within: A revolutionary understanding of happiness and fulfillment

The Art of Relationship: Secrets of Long Lasting Fulfilling Relationships

Positive Thinking: What It Really Takes To Free Yourself From Negativity

The sole purpose of the book *Positive Thinking* is to help readers shift to a more optimistic, positive thinking mindset in order to attain happiness and fulfillment in life.

The author struggled with habitual negative thoughts & low self-esteem for thirteen years. His tussle with negativity drove him to the world of human psychology and behavioral science. But something was missing. Happiness and positivity still eluded him. It was not a complete solution.

His search for an answer led him to eastern philosophy. Thousands of years old wisdom perfectly complemented modern day science. Combining the two, he was able to change himself from gloomy & pessimistic to an optimistic person.

Positive Thinking contains the most important thoughts and concepts that helped him shift his own mindset. Several myths about negative and positive thinking are debunked, guiding the reader through what really works by taking a realistic and practical approach.

End negativity and bring change at the deepest level.

Because negativity is a product of multiple issues functioning under the surface, the subject of negative and positive thinking has been broken into multiple levels. Readers are taken on a journey through "building self-belief" to "improving their health & mindset" to "finding happiness within ourselves".

What you will learn inside *Positive Thinking*?

- How to stop taking things personally?
- How to stop depending on situations & people for happiness?
- How to change the way you see the world?
- How your physical health changes your thoughts?
- How to believe in yourself & raise your self-esteem?
- How to guard your mind against negative influences?
- How to live worry free and enjoy the present moment?
- How to diminish your worst fears?
- How to create happiness and fulfillment in your relationships?

If you aim to move towards positive thinking, happiness, and high self-esteem... you must read this book.

The Happiness Edge: The Eight Principles of Happiness to Gain Competitive Advantage in Business and Life

What if you don't feel happy even after achieving success?

For generations, we have been taught that when we become successful, we'll be happy. If we can just make more money, or find an attractive partner, or get a six-pack, we'll be happy. Success equals happiness.

The recent advancements in the field of psychology suggest otherwise. We have to first become happier in order to achieve the next level in any endeavor.

The increase in happiness has been proven to facilitate clear thinking, more income, healthier relationships, increased motivation, and better health.

In *The Happiness Edge*, Vishal Pandey shares how happiness still eluded him even after achieving the life of his dreams. His quest to gain a deeper understanding of happiness led him to the field of psychology and related studies to discover secrets hidden in plain sight.

Backed up by several pieces of research conducted all over the world, *The Happiness Edge* presents eight groundbreaking principles of happiness which made a radical shift in the life of the author and the people he shared them with.

Discover:

- How to use apply the principle of *Core Element* to increase presence, joy, and productivity?

- How to change everything in your life and business using *The Law of Least Effort*?

- How to train your mind to become more accustomed to health, wealth, happiness, and prosperity by exercising the principle of *Calculated Influence*?

- 51 simple ways to make your life happier.

- And much more.

A must-read by anyone looking to utilize the power of happiness to reach the next level, or simply increase the amount of happiness you experience in a day. By leveraging the eight principles, along with 51 simple but effective ways to increase happiness, you can completely transform the way you think, live, and work.

Printed in Great Britain
by Amazon